The Junk that Challenged the Yachts

By Paul Chow

Norm:
At sea I had the
best shipmates.
At Porter Range
I have the best
neighbor
Paul

5/28/11

THE JUNK THAT CHALLENGED THE YACHTS. Copyright
© May 2011 Paul Chow

ISBN: 1461189152
EAN-13: 978-1461189152

Manufactured in the United States of America.

Dedicated To

My wife Vera

my children Maria, Theresa, Teh-han, Laura

and

my grandchildren Jessica, Jennifer, Melissa,

Ethan and Matthew

Acknowledgments

On behalf of my shipmates Marco Yu-Lin Chung, Loo-Chi Hu, Reno Chia-Lin Chen, Benny Chia-Cheng Hsu and Calvin E. Mehlert, I would like to take this belated opportunity to thank the people of Taiwan, particularly those names mentioned in this book, for supporting us in this project fifty-six years ago. I would like to thank Jo Fergerson Zhou and Jennifer Chiu for editing.

The Junk that Challenged

the Yachts

I

The storm finally gathered enough strength to whip the sea into furious white rollers. Fishing was good. But the boat was rolling so heavily during the last haul-up that half of our catch was washed off the deck. We tied everything down and made a run for shelter.

Sailing abreast of us was a junk, heading for the same place. We had the throttle of our 300 HP diesel engine wide open. She had all her sails fully spread to the tops of her two masts. By the time we reached the sheltered cove, the junk had already dropped her anchor. Her sails were neatly furled and her crew was swabbing the deck.

I wished some day I could set foot on one of those junks to feel that silent power of nature.

Then one day, I saw the following news in The China Post.

NEW YORK HERALD TRIBUNE - *In commemoration of the 125th Anniversary of the Royal Swedish Yacht Club, the New York Yacht Club announces that it will jointly sponsor a trans-Atlantic yacht race with the Swedes next summer. The race will start from Newport, Rhode Island on June 11, 1955 and finish in Gothenburg, Sweden for a gala celebration.*

Not too many readers could have noticed it. It was hidden in a corner on the last page. Even if someone did, it would probably not raise any eyebrow. The Atlantic Ocean was so far away. A yacht race was so far fetched for the Chinese mind. Very few people here had ever heard of yachts, let alone seeing one. Boats in China were for transportation and fishing only, not for sports or pleasure. Besides, in this part of the world, sports were to be participated, not watched or read about. But it sure popped open my eyes.

If the North Atlantic is as stormy as it is reputed for, I thought, I bet a junk can easily beat those fancy yachts on those rough waters.

I was thinking of the junk that beat me to shelter in that storm many years ago. I had fished with these junks in sight for so many years in all kinds of weather. As a result, I had developed a lot of respect and admiration toward them. Having lost a boat in a typhoon later and now being stranded ashore, I couldn't help but dream about them like stranded seafarers dreaming about the sea gulls. My thought unconsciously slipped out of my mouth,

"Will they let a junk join this yacht race?"

All the heads in the apartment turned around and gave me a funny look. No one made any comment though. But a little while later, I heard someone say,

"Why don't you ask them?"

"Who are they?" I asked.

"Those who sponsor the race," said Reno.

That made sense. I immediately dashed off a letter of inquiry. The best address I could gather from the announcement to put on the envelope was:

New York Yacht Club
c/o New York Herald Tribune
New York City, U.S.A.

That night, that junk which raced me in the storm came back to me in my dream. Only this time it took place on the Atlantic Ocean and I was holding her tiller in my hands.

When I did not hear anything for two weeks, I started to get nervous. Two weeks should be plenty time for them to give me a response. Perhaps the letter got lost. Did I have enough information in the address? Perhaps they thought I was joking.

"A junk in a yacht race? You got to be joking!" Even my apartment mates thought so. None of them was supportive to my idea. One discouragement after another was hurled at me.

"Yacht races are rich people's games, not for a poor Chinese fisherman like you," said Marco.

"Junks are designed to work, not to race," Benny reminded me.

"You wouldn't have a Chinaman's chance, as they say in America, even if you get accepted," Reno added. "Besides, what do you know about sailboats? Where are you going to find a junk crew to sail for you?"

Their comments did not discourage me. They only led me to think about it in a more practical sense. How could a junk with patched sails and a blunt bow beat those slick looking racing yachts with pointed swallow-like white sails and slender shark-like bodies? I tried to think of some circumstance that could put the junks at an advantageous position. As Benny had pointed out, junks were designed for work and yachts for pleasure. So junks could probably take the rough weather much better than yachts. Junks did not have the luxury of radio. When a typhoon hit, they had only one choice - ride it out. As a result, all junks that had survived on the China coast would have gone through many typhoons that ran up the China coast many times a year. Suppose the race ran into one of them. Do they have typhoons on the Atlantic?

That night I dreamed of sailing in a storm. I dreamed of some yacht losing her mast. I dreamed of myself being torn between sailing on to win the race and going to the rescue of my competitor.

Two months had passed. There was still no news. My anxiety slowly waned out. Gradually the flying sails, the stormy sea, the race and the junk... all faded into a misty fog.

II

I walked into the port captain's office one morning. The office girl who took care of the mails showed me a telegram in English and asked.

"Who is this addressed to?"

I'll be... It was my name!

I held it in my hand and did not know what to do with it. In China no one sent a telegram unless it was a matter of life or death, something like "Grandpa passed away last night". When I finally gathered enough courage to open it, these words jumped out in front of my eyes:

WE ARE GLAD TO ACCEPT YOUR JUNK TO THE RACE STOP YOU ARE ASSIGNED RACING NUMBER 320 STOP LETTER IN DETAILS TO FOLLOW STOP OCEAN RACE COMMITTEEE CHAIRMAN NEW YORK YACHT CLUB G W BLUNT WHITE STOP

So far all I had was a faded dream. I had to read the telegram aloud several times to convince myself that I was not in a dream. When I was finally jolted back to reality, I realized that there was no such junk as mentioned in the telegram.

It was already November. June was only seven months away. If I were serious, I must find a junk and get her over there within that time.

Rhode Island was two oceans away. Junks were for coastal sailing only. How was I going to fit an old junk for ocean sailing? A whole bunch of questions immediately came to my mind one after another.

Where could I get sailing charts for foreign waters? China did not even print charts for her own coast.

How was I supposed to learn how to handle a sailboat? My experience was limited to diesel fishing boats only.

How was I going to navigate on open waters? In fishing we could be out of the sight of land only for days, not for weeks or months. We could easily run dead reckoning from one landmark to another. On the ocean there were thousands of miles of open waters where we could see nothing but stars and sun.

Then how could I get a passport? Only those on official business or students to study abroad were issued passports.

How could I get an exit permit? Since Martial Law was instated, the draft age was extended to 40. I was only 28.

How could I get a sailing permit for a junk? All sea-going vessels in Taiwan, including sailing vessels, were regimented into a civilian fleet so that in the event when the Nationalists decided to launch an invasion on the Communist occupied Mainland, every single vessel on the island could be mobilized as a part of the attack force.

Finally, where could I find money to buy a junk?

I dug up whatever I had saved during my nine years of fishing. Some were in silver dollars and some in small gold rings. (In Taiwan, we trusted neither the local New Taiwan Currency nor the banks. All commodity prices were gauged in American dollars. People hid their valuables under their beds.) I counted an equivalence of US$850.

I knew that if I tried to solve these problems all at once, I would never get started. First thing first, I must find a junk.

Getting a junk should not be a problem. As described in China Coast Pilot published by the most recent edition of British Royal Navy:

Junks are part of the coastal scene of China just like sea gulls are to a fishing harbor. When approaching the China Coast, sailing junks will be sighted before any sign of land. Wherever they are there will be safe waters.

It was not too many years ago that the Japanese had

5

mechanized all the fishing boats in Taiwan during their occupation. So if there were any junks left in Taiwan, they must be abandoned on beaches. I changed all my silver dollars and gold rings into American dollars. With $850 in my pocket I set off on a junk hunt.

After searching all the beaches and rivers around Northern Taiwan, I found only one junk, sitting high and dry on the bank of the Tamsui River outside of Taipei. Its bottom was cracked; its masts were turned into flagpoles; its topside was colorfully painted and decorated with a sign: "The Floating Teahouse".

Shucks!

In dashed hope, I abandoned my search. I took the last train to Taipei. When I got there, it was already close to curfew time. All connecting train and buses had stopped running. I had no way to get back to where I lived, Keelung. So I went to spend the night at a friend's place.

We have a saying in Chinese: Bad luck never strikes alone. At about two o'clock in the morning, the police raided my friend's place in search of underground Communists. Under the Martial Law, all residences in Taiwan were subject to unannounced search once a month. Any Communist found would face the firing squad, some without trials.

While the place was searched, its residents were lined up to have their identification papers checked. When they came to me, they found out that I had not registered at the police station to stay there overnight. I was immediately hauled away and thrown into the city jail. I stayed in the crowded cell with thugs and thieves until the court convened in the morning. I suddenly remembered the "fighting Communists, resisting Russia" slogans that we were supposed to quote from time to time and to mimic in public. In court I let them out of my mouth. I recited them with such ferventness that I impressed the judge right away that I could not a Communist. After paying a three-silver-dollar fine, I was freed.

I had nothing to complain about the incident except my own carelessness. How I wished that I could go back to sea, where I would not have to be subject to all this nonsense.

December came. I still did not have a junk. Perhaps if I had a crew, we could comb all the beaches on the island rather than just around the northern part like what I had done. But how could I convince anyone to join me? They had to be as crazy as I was. All I could promise them was a dream and all I could show them was a piece of wrinkled yellow paper from America.

III

It turned out that finding a crew was much easier than finding a junk. There were enough crazy people among my friends. The first one that came to my mind was Huloo.

Huloo was good with nets. I figured that sails and nets were very similar. One sailed in air and one sailed in water. They both tried to spread out as much as they could. The only difference was one tried to catch air and one tried to catch fish.

Huloo had always argued that fish would eventually be raised in confined space for food like in animal husbandry rather than be caught in the wild. So he quit fishing a year ago and came ashore to try to raise freshwater eel in ponds. He was so successful that he turned an experiment that the Japanese had tried unsuccessfully for many years into a moneymaking business.

"I quit the sea for good when I quit fishing," he said to me when I told him of my idea. "Besides, I have no interest in racing nor any desire to go to America."

"I didn't know you hated the sea so much," I said.

"But if you want to do it, I'll go along just to help you out. I know you have always wanted to go to America."

"You could say that before I got this idea of sailing a junk on an ocean," I admitted. "To tell you the truth, after spending nine years in fishing, I was also beginning to get tired of it like you. You go to raise eel. For me, going to America was the only way to get out of it. Look, this island is only so big. What chance does an uneducated fisherman have to compete for a shore job with those college graduates?"

"Why America?"

"It's so big and has so few people."

"Why not go get a college degree? Then you would be among the few."

"I tried. They would not even let me take the entrance exam."

"Why?"

"Because they said I have not finished high school."

"Then finish high school."

"I don't need to. The yacht race will free me from everything, high school, college and jobs. After the race, I will sail around the world to visit all those places that I have dreamed about since I was a child."

"Where are you going to find money to do that?"

"Why would I need money? The junk doesn't consume anything. For me, all I need is food. That I could fish. As about America, it doesn't matter any more. Look, the final destination of the race is Sweden, not America. The world is much more interesting than America."

"Sweden or America, whatever you say. I don't mind to go take a look at a new place." I was surprised that Huloo did not put up an argument with me as he used to do.

Then I told him I needed to find four more people to go with me.

"Why so many?" he asked. "Just you and I can handle it comfortably. To tell you the truth, I can do it all by myself. It's just another outing in the countryside." That sounded typical Huloo. Everything in life was easy. He could do everything by himself, without helps from anyone.

"Look," I said. "I am going on this trip for fun, not to work my ass off. Fishing is over for me."

"Why six?"

"We need two on each watch. With six we only have to work eight hours a day, just like the people in the office."

"Whatever you say," Huloo surprised me again in not putting up an argument. "This is your junk and your adventure."

Did he call it adventure? I had been telling everybody that it was a yacht race. And all my apartment mates thought it was just my fantasy and I would eventually forget it. But when I showed them the invitation from the New York Yacht Club, they changed their minds right away. They all wanted to join.

Before we came to Taiwan, we were all fishermen in Shanghai. Huloo liked to figure out how things work. As a fisherman, he wanted to find out how fish think. So he had always been interested in different methods to catch them. When he learned that the Taiwanese fishermen had a new method to catch tuna, namely with thousands of hooks stringed up on a 15-mile long fish-line, he immediately asked for a transfer. I came because I was tired of fishing in the icy cold waters and wanted to seek a romantic life in the tropical waters for a change. Reno was in the middle of a hot poker game with some friend when their boat was pulling out to sea. He went along to finish the game. A few days later, he found himself in Taiwan. True or not, he never denied it when I told the story. He just listened and smiled. Benny came from a fishing village Swamei in South China. Seamen in China were clannish. Their associations were tightly knitted by the dialects they spoke. To get away from those older Ningpo fishermen who were constantly pulling rank over him, he came to Taiwan, where the dialect was very similar to that spoken in his village. (The ancestors of Taiwanese came from Amoy and Meihsien, which were very close to Swatow and Swamei.) Marco was from the north. He went to Shanghai to bring a modern steel diesel trawler back to his homeport, Tsingtao. Before 1946, all fishing boats in China were made of wood and powered by wind. Then on the eve of the Communist takeover of the city, his boat was seized by the Nationalist secret police and he ended up in Taiwan.

I needed one more. I asked Chiang.

Chiang was my skiff mate. In the previous summer when my boat was hauled up on the slipway to have her annual bottom scraping and engine overhaul, I got nothing to do. So I persuaded Chiang to join me in trying to rig up my skiff as a sailboat. The skiff was never able to sail. But our friendship flew. This time I did not need to twist his arms. All I said was "Here is another chance for you and I to rig a sail on a sailboat. The difference is this time we will definitely sail."

Here we were, the crew of the phantom junk that existed only in our fantasy:

Hu, Loo-Chi (Huloo), born and raised in Shanghai

Chen, Chia-Lin (Reno), born and raised in Shanghai

Chung, Yu-Lin (Marco), born and raised in Peiping

Hsu, Chia-Cheng (Benny), born and raised in Guangdong

Chiang, Huai-Ren, born in Hunan, grew up in Chungking

Myself, Chow, Chuan-Juin (Paul), born in Peiping to father from Canton, mother from Shanghai, ancestors from Shandong and raised in different places throughout China

We were all 28-year-old except Huloo, who was two years older. We were all single and had been fishing boat captains at one time or another except Chiang, who was a marine engineer, married and had a wife and a daughter. For one reason or another, we were all stranded ashore.

IV

We had one more thing in common. None of us had ever set foot on any sailboat before. That aroused a lot of skepticism among people we knew.

"Do you really know what you are getting into?" they all asked the same question.

"No." We had no idea of what it was going to be like. We were coastal fishermen. None of us had ever sailed on an open ocean. But we were all determined to make our dream real. To be realistic, perhaps we should test our ability in how to cope with unexpected situations before plunging into the unknown. I proposed a bicycle trip across Taiwan. There were 380 kilometers of hilly roads from the northern tip of the island to its southern tip. None of us had seen any part of it except on a train. None of us had ever pedaled a bike for more than five miles at a time inside the city. Having spent so many years at sea without using our legs, they had probably regressed to that of a frog. All these conditions should make the ride a good test.

But not all my fellow dreamers were keen on the idea.

"Eh, what does riding a bicycle have to do with sailing a junk?" Reno asked. Reno was a city person. He tried to stay as far away as possible from any kind of physical exertion. The only "sport" he would consider participating in was on the pool table. Sailing was fine. The deck was like a pool table. He did not need to run or lift any weight.

Chiang told me that ever since he joined us, his wife had become withdrawn and somewhat hysterical in behavior. "She'll be all right," he said. "It's just a matter of getting used to the idea. I think I had better stay home to work on that."

Benny always had a romantic feeling about the unpredictability of fishermen's life. He was often engrossed in dreaming about how people would remember him after he was lost at sea. His most favorable icon was the fishermen's monument in Gloucester with the inscription "They that Go Down the Sea in Ships". To Benny, the junk trip would be the ultimate romantic adventure of life, a venture sailing into the unknown. He thought there was a great chance that we might not come back. So he thought he should spend as much time as he could with his former marine college principal's daughter, whom he had a crush on but did not have the courage to tell her his feeling. "Perhaps now is the time," he said.

Marco was a typical northerner, big, strong and steadfast with the endurance of a camel that one often saw on the Peiping streets, which was forever on the move with steady steps and a heavy load. He had such a good nature that he would go along with anybody.

So my bicycle trip ended up with just the three of us, Huloo, Marco and I.

I borrowed a bike without any reduction gears. To avoid the subtropical heat of Taiwan, we started in the late afternoon and planned on riding through the night. An hour after leaving Keelung, we ran into the afternoon traffic of Taipei. While the traffic in Keelung was mostly bicycles and petticabs, the traffic in Taipei was predominantly motor vehicles: public busses, private cars, army trucks and American jeeps with bicycles, petticabs and oxcarts filling in the cracks. We were overwhelmed by the confusion. In no time we were separated from each other. Two hours later Huloo and I rejoined. But we lost Marco.

Not too long into the ride, my legs got tired. Then came the pains and the cramps. Before we covered half of the journey, my legs became totally numb. I started to look forward to the curfew law, under which no one was supposed to be out on the street after midnight. That would give us a break. But to my great disappointment, there was no one to enforce it on the highway. In thinking back, we were fortunate that it did not happen. Otherwise we would never have been able to get back on our bikes after a break. The 380-kilometer ride took us 21 hours. During the last few hours, I did not even know whether my legs were attached to my body or to the bicycle. When we arrived at our destination, our legs were so stiff that we had to fall off our bikes to dismount.

Marco was waiting for us there.

"Congratulations for breaking the record of the slowest speed in bicycle riding," he said.

"When did you get here?"

"This morning."

"I see that big body does count. We almost didn't make it."

"That mountain road between Taipei and Taichung was a killer. I figured that you guys would not have made it. So after the climb, I put my bike on the train and came down here, ha, ha, ha, ha..."

"You son-of-a-gun!" I was surprised that I still had the strength to curse him. "But to be honest, I have been thinking about doing the same thing all through the ride."

"Then why didn't you quit?"

"I was waiting for Huloo to suggest it."

"You bi-yang-de!" cursed Huloo. "I have been waiting for you to suggest it!"

"You too?" I asked.

"Because I could not stand seeing you suffer with so much pain."

"Sure. Now you still think you can sail solo across the ocean?"

"I can. I don't know about you though."

That was typically Huloo! The thing was he probably could and would force himself to do it. But for me, I realized for the first time that companionship was as important as physical stamina, probably even more.

Before we left on our bicycle trip, a reporter from Central News, Song Yue, showed up at our apartment. He said he had heard about our proposed voyage and wanted to write a feature story about it. I had no idea how he had heard about us and I did not care about his feature story either. I refused. My mother had told me to avoid four kinds of people: lawyers, politicians, newspaper reporters and prostitutes. But he kept showing up at our apartment every morning. (There was no door or doorbell to our apartment. Anybody could just walk in.) I did not want to throw him out or be rude to him because my mother had warned me, "Watch out for the reporters. They talk sweet. But they can ruin your life." So I just ignored him politely.

When we returned to Keelung on the next day, there he was again.

"Your riding across Taiwan on bikes will be a nice lead to your Pacific Crossing on a junk," Mr. Song said to me. "Let me write a story about it and get it published in Central News."

I told him I had a lot of things to take care of and I did not have any time to sit down and talk to him.

"I can just tag along and ask you some questions."

"Why should I have my story appear in a newspaper?" Finally I could not hide my contempt any longer.

"It can help you."

"How can news help?"

"I can tell my readers that you are still looking for a junk."

"So they all know about it. What can they do?"

"Someone may just have seen one somewhere."

"I have traveled all over the northern Taiwan coast and did not see a single junk except that floating restaurant on the bank of Tamsui River. Now you are telling me that some of your readers may have seen one?" I asked.

I still believed my mother was right about these press people. All they wanted was a story to sell their papers. They would say anything to get it. They couldn't care less about the outcome or what harm it would bring to their subjects. I walked away without giving him an answer. But the next day, a story about our bicycle ride and six young men's dream of sailing in a yacht race appeared in Central News.

V

The rain in Keelung fell more than three hundred days out of a year. That restrained us from all the outdoor activities. As we were cooped up in the apartment one rainy afternoon doing nothing, a green Oldsmobile pulled up in front of the house. Passenger cars were rare in Keelung. One with a color other than black was even rarer. That stirred up quite a commotion in the neighborhood. A gentleman in a Western sport jacket got out and came into our apartment. He introduced himself as the head of the Chinese Red Cross, Dr. Liu Rui-Heng. He said he had read in an English newspaper about a person in Keelung by the name of Paul Chow who had entered a Chinese junk in an international yacht race. I told him there was no junk.

"That's what the paper said," he said. "I just couldn't believe anyone crazy enough to enter a yacht race without a boat. I had to meet this person."

I told him I did search the harbors and beaches. But I could not find a single junk. "However, a Navy officer told me that he had seen lots of them in Tachen," I said.

"You mean that island off the Mainland coast that is still in Kuomintang's hand?" he asked. "Did you go take a look?"

"No. It is a military base. No civilian is allowed."

"That shouldn't be a problem," the gentleman said. "I can talk to your mayor. I know Mr. Hsie Guan-Yi very well. We went to school together in Michigan. The northern branch of the Navy is based right in his city. I'm sure he can get you a ride on one of those Navy ships."

Early next morning I got a message from the mayor asking me to go see him. When I saw him, he told me that he had already talked to the Garrison Headquarters and the Navy.

"How many of you are going?" he asked. "They need your names."

I gave him Huloo's name and mine.

"Just two?" he asked in surprise. "How are you going to get the junk back to Keelung once you find one?"

"It's just a short hop across the Taiwan Strait," I told him. "We will manage."

"Have you sailed a junk before?" he asked in concern.

"No. But we are fishermen."

"Aren't the fishing boats powered by diesel engines rather than sails?"

"All boats are more or less the same, Mr. Mayor," I assured him. "Once you know how to sail one, you sort of know how to handle all of them. Don't worry. Before taking her out to sea we will make sure that the owner of the junk shows us all the ins and outs on how to handle the sails."

The mayor nodded thoughtfully. I assumed that my explanation had satisfied him. Luckily there was no one in that office that knew anything about boats.

We boarded a Navy LSM (Landing Ship Medium) at the Navy pier. We were met by her captain at the gangway. "We do not have passenger accommodation on this bucket," he warned us. "You guys can stay in the officers' mess hall. The good thing is it is next to the galley which is the warmest place on the whole ship."

For the entire week following that we never left the mess hall. We never saw Tachen either. On the second day out at sea, the Communists mounted an attack on a small island, Yijiangshan, next to Tachen. Since the LSM was not a combat ship, she was ordered to stand by at a distance away from the battle for emergency evacuation if necessary. It had never become necessary. Yijiangshan was lost to the Communist at the end of a bloody battle. All the defenders were killed. So was our hope in finding a junk.

VI

There was not a single word exchanged between Huloo and I from the time the LSM headed back a home. As we entered the breakwater of the Keelung Harbor, Huloo broke the silence, "I know this is like the end of the world for you. But for me, it is just like the cancellation of a fishing trip or a bicycle trip. I'll just go back to Taoyuen to raise more eel. You should do the same. Go back to fishing."

I did not respond.

As the LSM was maneuvering into the Navy Pier, we noticed something sticking up against the backdrop of a row of dilapidated warehouses across the harbor. They looked like ship's masts. But they were too short for a cargo ship and too bare for a fishing boat. Could it be a...?

We hurriedly disembarked and rushed across the harbor. Behind a row of tall warehouses, there she was, a junk bobbing up and down on the waves generated by passing ships. She had two bulging eyes the size of big watermelons gawking at us above a green bushy whisker. Her hull was bare and dry like firewood. Her deck was cracked. Her two masts were standing without any support like tree trunks after a forest fire. One of them was leaning at an angle, ready to fall. At the foot of each mast there was a huge bundle of bamboo poles wrapped in some tan colored rags. There was a cabin behind the mainmast. On the front of the cabin there was a wooden plate. Three characters, *Sheng Shiao Li,* were carved on it. These words (meaning *Winning, Piety and Profit)* did not make any sense to me. They could mean to bring luck or they could be the junk's name.

We hailed. No one responded. We went on board and peeped

into the cabin. We saw an old man sitting on a platform in the dark all by himself. We could not understand what he was saying when we asked him where the owner of the junk was. All we could figure out was he was speaking in the Foochow dialect. We rushed back to our fishing boats and returned with a fisherman who could speak the dialect. Through our interpreter we found out that the junk came into port with a shipload of salt fish from Foochow just a few days ago. The old man was not the owner. He was the *laoda* (the old man or the skipper). The owner, Lian Yi-Kwai, had gone ashore to look for buyers for his cargo the minute the junk docked. He had not been seen since then.

"When do you expect him to show up back on the junk?" I asked. The *laoda* spread out his hands and said. "Who knows? He is a big gambler."

With the clue I got from the *laoda*, I went to look for the owner of the junk in every underground gambling den. Gambling was illegal in Taiwan. I was directed from one to another. When I finally found him, he had not slept for three days and was short tempered. He had been losing heavily. He had gambled away his cargo at a cut price and was agonizing in whether or not to put his junk up as a stake. My offer to buy the junk came just in time. He asked for 40,000 yuan in the New Taiwan Currency. That was equivalent to US$1000! I had no idea whether that was a fair price or not. As far as I was concerned, that was my last chance to get hold of a junk. I agreed.

But I must find $150 more to make up the $1000 payment for the junk. I also needed more to cover what would be needed to refit her for a long ocean voyage and to buy spare ropes and provision for the crew.

"Go sell everything you have to the consignment stores," I told my crew. Consignment stores were like the pawnshops in the old days. After the government barred the import of foreign goods, they popped up everywhere.

But no one did. I had been counting on Marco's tailored suits. He liked to dress. But he told me he had given them all to his brother-in-law's brother-in-law. Benny had a bicycle. He claimed that he had promised it to the brother of his "girlfriend". I knew I could not squeeze anything from Reno. His only possession was the clothes on his body and a few under his mattress for change. Only Huloo had some savings that I could possibly tap on.

All this time, Song Yue, the reporter from Central News, was tagging along after me. He was there when I asked the crew to sell their possessions. On the next morning, a news item appeared on Central News describing our fruitless trip to Tachen and the accidental discovery of the Sheng Shiao Li. At the end of the article he commented, "But these young ocean adventurers are still short of 6,000 yuan to pay for the junk."

Just after I had borrowed 6,000 yuan from Huloo, I received a message from the Mayor of Keelung. He asked me to go to his office.

"I heard that you are short of 6,000 yuan for buying the junk," the Mayor said to me. "Tell you what, I'll go fifty-fifty with you. I will chip in 20,000 yuan if you call it City of Keelung."

It was like money falling from sky. How could the name of a junk worth that much? She was definitely not a new-born baby to a grandfather. As a matter of fact, I had been having difficulty in picking a name.

Dragon Seed was one that first came to my mind. Dragon was the symbol of China. Seed was the young generation. But then it had already been used as the name of a book written by a foreigner, Pearl Buck. I wanted something real Chinese. Actually her present name Sheng Hsiao Li was very Chinese. But it sounded business and smelled money and carried no real meaning.

What's the big deal about a name? I accepted the Mayor's offer right away.

I knew it would take ages to have the check request to be covered with red seals of approvals from those bureaucrats before it became official, even though it was initiated from the mayor's office. I did not have the luxury of time. So instead of waiting for the check, I went to a lawyer, Mr. Lin Fang, to have him draw out a sales contract for me right away. When he learned that I was going to sail a junk across the Atlantic Ocean, he waived his fee.

"Consider it a small contribution from me to satisfy my father's will," he said. "You see, the name my father gave me, Fang, means boat. But I have never set foot on any boat in my life."

It boosted my morale more than it helped my financial situation. I had not realized that I had so many supporters.

With two copies of the drafted sales contract and 34,000 yuan in the New Taiwan Currency that I had got from exchanging my US$850 plus 6,000 yuan from Huloo, I went back to the junk owner. I handed him my entire life's saving plus some from Huloo in a bundle wrapped in newspaper and said,

"Here you are, all 40,000 of it. Count it."

He looked at the bundle and did not show any inclination to open it. "That's not enough," shaking his head he said.

"What? You didn't even count it."

"The price is 46,000 yuan."

"But you told me 40,000!"

"That was three days ago. Now it's 46,000."

I asked him why. He would not give me an answer. He just said,

"46,000. Take it or leave it."

VII

Come to think of it, with the Mayor's pledge of 20,000 yuan, what was another 6,000? I borrowed another 6,000 from Huloo and rushed back to the junk owner lest he should change his mind and raise the price again. After he counted the money, he said to me as if he had been shortchanged, "You'll find this price dirt cheap when you sell her in America."

So that was why he raised the price! That son-of-a-bitch! He called it profit sharing?

As I was getting the transaction paper in order, the Mayor asked me to go see him again. In his office he told me he was withdrawing his pledge.

I did not know what to say.

It turned out that the governor of Taiwan, Yen Chia-Gan, had called him up and told him that he would like to buy the junk for us. The mayor thought it would be a better deal for us. He figured we could save our money to buy provisions and to pay for the repairs. "The Governor's only request is that you call the junk *Free China*," the Mayor told me.

I could not understand why would these officials bidding against each other for a name. It was the least concern of ours. Without hesitating a second, I accepted the Governor's offer. When I received the check from the Governor, I asked the officer who handed me the check whether I should put the Governor's name or the Provincial Government of Taiwan as the owner of the junk in the new registration.

"Neither," the officer said to me. "Look, the junk will be a liability to anybody who owns it. The government certainly does not want to assume such a headache. That is why the Governor gives you only 45,000 so that by paying the difference of 1,000 yuan you can claim the title."

Me, the owner of a US$1250 yacht? How many people in China could afford to own a yacht?

For a long time I could not believe it. All I had ever owned in my life before was a typewriter, a phonograph, some long play records and my clothes could be fitted into one sea bag. I did not even own a bicycle like Benny and Huloo did.

The Sheng Shiao Li was a Foochow pole junk, which was originally designed to carry lumbers. Pole junks were otherwise known as *Ping-tou* (Flat Head) for having flat bows above the waterline or as *Hua-pi-gu* (Flowery Fanny) for having their fantails painted with flowery designs.

The Surveying Certificate issued by the Keelung Harbor Authority in 1952 showed the following measurements:

Length total: 24.25 meters

Length at line of tonnage calculation: 19.13 meters

Beam: 5.40 meter

Draft: 1.48 meters

Tonnage below deck: 20.25 metric tons

Tonnage above deck: 1.33 metric tons

Crew's quarters: -1.80 metric tons

Total tonnage: 19.78 metric tons

Other measurements not listed in the certificate included:

Number of holds: 11

Number of masts: 2

Length of mainmast: 18 meters

Length of foremast: 11.6 meters tilted 25° forward from the plumb line

Area of the mainsail: 180 square meter

Area of foremast: 80 square meter

Size of rudder (under the keel): 1 meter x 4 meter

The registration showed that she was launched in 1949. But she looked so old and so weather beaten. There were cracks everywhere, even inside the cabin. No one could believe that she was only six years old. The former owner must have lied. But there was nowhere to check. She was built in Foochow on the Mainland but the registration was issued by the Keelung Harbor Office. No one had seen her original paper that was issued in Foochow because she was caught smuggling opium and confiscated by the Taiwanese Customs. When she was auctioned off, the new owner got a new registration and new name for her. Not as men, who always tried to register their age older than they really were to avoid drafting, new owners always registered their boats younger so that they could boost up their resale values.

Being old was one thing. But being unseaworthy was totally another thing. When we went through the junk, we immediately found out that there was a lot of work needed to be done before we could take her to sea. The former owner had not kept up with the maintenance. The Mayor was right. The repair would require a lot of money. Only then were we so thankful to the Governor for giving us that bulk of money.

We hired a junk-wright from Foochow, Ou Ah-Lin, to do the repairs. He looked as old as the junk and had lost an eye and several teeth. But we could not be choosy. Junks were hard to come by in this mechanized age. Junk-wrights were even harder to come by. We were lucky to find one.

The old sails were made of some flimsy material and patched over and over again with flour sacks and rags. We definitely needed a new set. There were two of them, foresail and mainsail, measuring a total of 2,200 square feet. None of us was good in needlework. So we hired some professional canvas sewers. We did not throw away the old sails. We put them in the hold as spares. We also ordered a set of bamboos enough to make a whole new set of battens. That occupied half of the deck space on the fore deck.

We paid the junk's *laoda* (skipper) to stay on with us until our departure to show us how to handle the junk.

"You can't handle it," was the first thing the *laoda* said to us.

"Why?" we were stunned. Now that he was paid as an adviser, he talked like an adviser.

"She requires a crew of fourteen. There are only six of you."

"Why fourteen?"

"You need six on each scull and one on the tiller and one book keeper."

"We are not going to scull on the ocean! And we don't need a book keeper."

"Then thirteen. You need twelve to raise the sail and one *laoda* on the tiller."

"We can use a tackle to raise the sail." That shut his mouth but not his head. It kept shaking.

We rigged up a triple-block tackle to be tied on the mast top. But when we tried to raise the sail with its gaff and eight bamboo battens, we could barely do it. When it got wet, we realized, it would weigh more than double. We found a hand-cranked winch discarded by one of the fishing boats. It did the job but it took forever to crank the sail 60 feet up on the mast. We needed a small donkey engine.

Since the junk was designed for coastal sailing, the original water tank was definitely not big enough for our purpose. I had four new wooden water tanks built in two of the cargo holds.

The junk normally carried 20 tons of cargo. But we would be sailing without any cargo. That meant her center of gravity would be higher than normal. That could pose some danger of capsizing when under sail. I ordered 5 tons of cobblestones to be distributed among the cargo holds as ballast. I also ordered 50 empty 50-gallon diesel drums to fill the empty space in her cargo holds.

"Why these drums?" asked Benny. "When I asked you to buy tools, you said we would never use them. Now you are wasting money on these empty drums that will absolutely serve no purpose."

"In case of a leak, they will keep the junk afloat," I explained.

"The junk is made of wood. It is unsinkable."

"Yes, it is made of wood. Why did you ask me to buy a complete set of machine tools?"

With wide opened eyes, a red face and swollen veins on his neck, he shut up and walked away.

All this time while I was preoccupied in finding a junk and a crew and in making the junk seaworthy, I had not given any thought on how to get from here to the race. Only now that I had a junk and a crew did I think of drawing a course for the voyage. I had never drawn any course for such a long voyage before. So I wrote to Capt. Bosshardt (Cap) for advice. He was our fishing fleet navigator. I owed all my knowledge in navigation to him.

Cap was a retired sea captain. He had sailed not only on big ocean-going steamships but also on tall ships with square-rigged sails that ran the China Trade between San Francisco and Shanghai. So I figured that he must know something about sailing.

Cap's response came very quickly. In his letter he pointed out:

"From where you are, the most direct route is to cross the Pacific Ocean. Once you reached the West Coast of America, all you have to do is to follow to coastline all the way to your destination. The shores are straight and the navigation lights and beacons are plentiful. You can stop anywhere to resupply your boat. I am sending you all the charts you will need and some weather charts. When you draw your course, try stay in the 40th parallel where you will find favorable westerly winds. But try to avoid the winter and spring months. Weather is very rough in those months in the North Pacific. I've seen many iron ships broken in half. If you come in June, July or August, you will certainly have God's providence."

But the race was scheduled to start in mid June. The shortest route between Keelung and our destination on the East Coast of America was 10,000 miles. Assuming a speed of 6 knots, it would take us 70 days to cover that distance. That meant we must leave here before April. We were on a race with time.

In Cap's letter he mentioned that he had seen many big iron ships broken in half. Then I got to thinking. When a ship broke up, what would the crew do? Wouldn't they get into smaller lifeboats? Does that mean that smaller boats could handle the rough seas better than the big ones? Fishermen never prayed for smooth sea. We could handle the rough weather. We just prayed for good fishing. Now all we prayed for was good wind.

I thought I had every little detail worked out. Then one day the director of the radio station for the fishing fleet, Mr. Lai Jun-Cheng, told me that we must have a two-way communication radio on board before we could get the sailing permit. "I have a marine radio transmitter, a Collins TCS-13 that was taken off an American landing ship," said Mr. Lai. "I have no use for it and you can have it. This machine only operates on Morse codes, not voice. What this means is that you guys must learn to communicate in Morse code and must pass the radio operator's test. No passing, no license. No license, no sailing permit."

"You all heard what Mr. Lai has just said," I turned to the crew and said. "No shore pass from now on. Everyone stays in the apartment in the evening to practice on the Morse code until we all pass the operator's test."

This was not all. The radio was run on batteries and the batteries needed to be charged. We definitely needed to find a small engine for charging the batteries.

I happened to see one in one of the import stores in Taipei. The store had a French name, Moulin. I walked into the store and was greeted by an elderly gentleman, Monsieur Lin Jun-Li. When I found out that he was educated in France, I tried my limited French on him. He immediately became exhilarated. When I told him that we were entering a Chinese junk into a trans-Atlantic yacht race and needed a small engine to do the work of raising the sail normally done by 12 men, he showed me a 5HP Danish diesel engine. "This is exactly what you want," he said. As I was looking over the engine with great interest, M. Lin seemed to be more interested in the junk trip. He kept on asking questions. When he found out that the junk was from Foochow, he said to me,

"I'm also from Foochow. Take it. No charge." When he saw the surprised expression on my face, he laughed and switched into French, "C'est un cadeau de la part d'un vieil homme qui voudrait vous accompagner dans ce voyage. Ne comprendez pas?"

VIII

On February 10 (121 days counting down to the start of the race) the owner of the Sheng Shiao Li, Lian Yi-Kwai, signed the junk to me in front of a notary public.

Assuming it would take us 70 days to get from here to the East Coast of America, we had only 51 days left to get the junk in shape and clear the bureaucracy for a sailing permit. On the very next day, I had the junk towed to the boatyard that belonged to Fishery Rehabilitation Administration (FRA) where she was hauled up on a slipway to have barnacles scraped off her bottom, whatever cracked seams calked and her entire body painted.

FRA was an agency established in early 1946 to rebuild China's war-torn fishing industry under a larger program administered by United Nations Relief and Rehabilitation Administration (UNRRA). It brought some two hundred diesel fishing boats to Shanghai, mostly from America and some from New Zealand, to be distributed to different parts of China. Up until then, the Chinese had been fishing exclusively on boats powered by wind. The fishermen must be trained before they could take over these motorized boats. All the UNRRA boats were manned by mixed crews, some the original crew who had brought the boats over and some the Chinese "trainees". To facilitate communication on board, an interpreter was put on each vessel. I was among the first applicants for that job.

There were four tables. At each table we were interviewed in a different dialect, one in Shandongese, one in Shanghainese, one in Cantonese and one in English. Each interviewer would then mark a pass or fail on our applications. I was a Shandongese, my mother was from Shanghai and I had gone to school in Canton during the first part of the Eight-year War with Japan and served in the army in Burma with the American soldiers during the last part of it. I had no trouble in getting passing marks at all the tables. I noticed that the applicant in front of me had only gotten two passing marks, one on Shanghai dialect and one on English. But when it came to having our salary bases assigned, I noticed that the Shanghai boy was assigned a salary base of 120 and I got only 70. Feeling I was being cheated, I asked for an explanation for the lower salary base given to me.

"He graduated from St. John's University," the man said. "You did not even finish high school."

What in the world does college have to do with being an interpreter for fishermen? I was so infuriated that I decided I would take on the world all by myself. I swore that I would never go to college, St. John's or any other, and I would show the world that I could do anything a college graduate could do and could do it better. I was nineteen then.

Six months later, the foreign fishermen were sent home. The boats were turned over to the Chinese fishermen. There was no more reason to keep the interpreters. I was dismissed. My mother thought that since I had had my fling, I should settle down and go to college.

But I had just gotten a taste of the sea. So instead of listening to my mother, I signed back up on the same fishing boat, this time as an apprentice. My salary base was cut in half to 35 and I would receive no bonus from the catch. I had to work the rope up from an apprentice to a fisherman and then to a mate. In three years I made captain and drew a salary base of 120, the same as that given to that St. John's graduate. But I had two shares, double that of a crew, of the bonus from the catch.

Now nine years later, I found myself back as an apprentice again. The difference this time was I must learn the ropes in two months instead of in three years. During these two months, I must learn from the *laoda* how to handle the junk; I must learn from One-Eye Ou Ah-Lin how to plug a leak and how to step a mast; I must learn from the sail makers to patch a tear and I must also

29

master the operation of sending and receiving radio messages in Morse code.

The first thing the *laoda* asked us to do was to memorize the names of all the ropes. We thought that was silly, particularly when we could not pronounce them in his Foochow dialect. We asked him to teach us how to handle the sail. We found that was totally impossible. He gave all the instructions in Foochow dialect, which we could not comprehend a single word of it. So we asked him to wait until we took the boat out for a shakedown cruise. Then he could show us with actions.

Morse code turned out to be the easiest thing to learn. There were only 26 codes for the alphabets and 10 for the numerals. But to achieve the speed required to pass the test took hours and hours of tedious practice. All six of us started. A week later I was the only one still tabbing on the key every evening. Did I like it? No. But if I quit, we would have no one to operate the radio. Without a radio operator, we would not be issued a sailing permit.

Everyone showed up at the boatyard when the junk was hauled up onto the slipway. Work stated immediately. Then someone noticed,

"Where is Marco?"

IX

Marco did not show up on the second day either. When I asked him when he would come to work on the junk, he said, "Tomorrow. I promise. Tomorrow." Tomorrow came. He said the same thing to me, "Tomorrow. I promise. Tomorrow."

Was he serious about this trip? His response to the bicycle ride had been more positive.

On the fourth day, my patience ran out. After everybody left the apartment, I confronted him, "How hard is it to part with that pretty mail girl in your office?"

"The Port Captain gives each boat only three days to stay in port. Within that time, I must supply them all what they have requested: water, fuel, nets, ropes, provisions, you name it."

"I can name more things that that need to be done on our junk. They can always find someone else to do these things in the office. It's a shore job. It's a fat job. There must be plenty of people lining up for it."

"Tomorrow. I promise. Tomorrow," he chuckled apologetically as he repeated his usual answer.

That was Marco, a nice guy, too nice to say no to anybody except his buddies. Actually I could find someone to take his place on the junk. Ever since we got the junk, we were bombarded with letters asking to join us. There were college students, schoolteachers, government employees, soldiers, seamen, professionals including a medical doctor and a deep-sea diver from Hong Kong. But I had told the crew that once they signed up, we would become equal partners in everything. "There will be no captain and no boss on this junk," I promised. "Every decision and action, including replacing a member of the crew, will be decided by the entire crew."

When Marco did not show up at the boatyard on the fifth day, I called a meeting.

"There are so many things to be done before we set sail," I said in dead seriousness. "We need every hand. We need to divide up the jobs among us. But firstly, let us elect a captain."

I was immediately reminded what I had said about no captain and no boss.

"I just learned that the sailing permit requires that we must have a captain." I was not bluffing. It was true, although the real purpose of calling the meeting was to get Marco to quit his job. "Besides, we need someone to serve as our spokesman." Huloo and I had talked about this earlier. We concluded that the only way to get Marco committed to the project was to elect him the captain. With Huloo's and my votes, we would need only one additional vote, which we were sure of getting. Both Huloo and I were very opinionated and abrasive in our manner of speech. Marco, on the other hand had the nicest personality and never raised his voice in opposition to anyone. "As far as the running of the junk is concerned, we will still go by votes," I assured the crew.

Everyone agreed. We held the meeting. At the end, we divided up the work and responsibilities among ourselves as follows:

Marco – captain, spokesman, buyer

Myself – navigator, radio operator, documents, food

Huloo – sail master, boatswain, doctor, barber

Reno – purser, liaison between hired workers and crew

Benny – carpenter, tools

Chiang – coxswain, engine, batteries

We added *buyer* to Marco's responsibility because, having worked so long in supplying the fishing boats, he knew quite a lot of ship chandlers and could probably get some good deals for us. Huloo was trained as a farmer before coming fishing. He had experience in castrating chicken, cats and dogs and shearing sheep. So we assigned him as our ship's doctor and barber in addition to his duty of taking care of the sails.

Just as Huloo and I had expected, Marco showed up at the boatyard the next morning. But we lost Chiang.

Chiang told us that lately his wife had had dreams of the junk going down at sea. She could not sleep, could not eat and was in tears every time she saw Chiang. Chiang figured that he would either go down with the boat (in his wife's mind) or lose his wife. He wanted out.

Instead of picking someone from our long application list, we asked a fellow fisherman of ours, Lin Feng-Chu, to join us. We must be careful this time, not to pick a married man. Lin was young, single, pleasant, physically strong, hard working, a good splicer, swift in the use of a (net) needle, graduated from a fishery school and had been fishing for three years. Most importantly, we knew him.

The first thing Lin did after joining us was to raise question on the height of the mast. "All those fishermen I know who have fished on junks before told me that our mast is too tall. We need to cut it down by at least three feet," he told us. We all thought he was crazy. Only Benny agreed with him.

"The mainmast does look too tall," Benny said. "None of the fishing junks my grandfather owned had such tall masts."

"That's ridiculous," said Reno. "The junk was not built yesterday. She must have gone through many storms, perhaps even some typhoons. Look, both masts are still standing."

"Have you ever set foot on a junk before?"

"Have you?"

"My grandfather used to own tens of these fishing junks."

"You did not answer my question."

Benny and Reno had been quarreling like this since their two fishing boats returned from their unsuccessful mullet fishing in Southern Taiwan. What had started it I did not know.

As far as Huloo and I were concerned, we did not give a damn how tall the mast was as long as we could have the entire sail spread out to catch wind. Marco did not offer any opinion. He never wanted to take sides in any argument. But if that would give Lin a peace of mind, we would cut it. We asked Ou Ah-Lin, the junk-wright, if he could have the mainmast shortened without making a big production.

"No problem," he said. "Let me show you how easy it is."

The hunch back junk-wright took off his shoes and climbed up the mainmast. He tied two ropes on its top. He had one rope run afore through the halyard block on the foremast and down to a block that was secured on deck. He had the other rope brought aft.

It was amazing to watch the one-eye junk-wright work. The mast was wedged in at the base between two sideboards and shored up by two fore-and-aft bearing sticks. Once the bearing sticks were removed, the mast became loose. He had his assistant hold on to the rope afore as he pulled on the rope astern. Lo and behold, the mast slowly fell aft and landed softly into the opening on the cabin as a sleeping baby being put into a cradle. After it was shortened, the mast went back up in reverse as easily as it came down, by being pulled on the rope afore with the rope astern guiding.

With the mainmast shortened, we thought Lin would feel at ease. But no, he acted more nervously. Pretty soon he started to lose sleep and lose weight. As the days went on, he had fewer and fewer words. All day long he mumbled to himself. At first we were too busy to pay any attention to him. Then one day he said to Benny, "The junk is going to go down."

"Every vessel would eventually go down, into the sea or into the ground," said Benny. "What else would you suggest we do? We have already shortened the mast as you have requested."

"She's just too old. According to what the junk-wright Ou Ah-Lin has estimated from the condition of the mast and planking, she must be over 50-year-old."

I had suspected that. I realized I was cheated when I paid 46,000 yuan for this piece of junk. It was dry like a bunch of firewood ready to go off with one strike of the match. But what could I have done? This was the only junk I could find. By this time, we were really teed off.

"She would get older if we waited longer," Reno told Lin.

"Since we cannot make her any younger," we finally told Lin. "We don't mind if you withdraw."

Lin quit the next day.

"It's good for everybody," said Marco. We did not want any one to sail with us with any kind of apprehension. "If he had said that earlier, we could have saved all that work done by Ou Ah-Lin."

"Even though Lin did not quit earlier," I said, "we could still have saved the mast from being cut."

"How?" all my fellow junk-mates turned to me and asked in disbelief.

"Put a clamp on the mast three feet below the top and then tie the top block of our halyard tackle on it. That would transfer off the force onto the clamp. All that extra mast above it would then become useless as if it had been cut off."

"Why didn't you say so before it was cut off?"

"I just thought of it now."

"Then keep it to yourself!"

Lin kept coming to the junk to help us on our work. He became very talkative. He even gained back the weight he had lost since coming on board the junk.

We did not fill Lin's vacancy. Who knows what the next person is going to be like? "What's the difference between five and six?" as Huloo said. "All we need is two to take turns at the tiller. Even for taking down the mast, you have seen how easily Ou Ah-Lin did it with just one helper."

With Lin gone, the job of running the 5HP donkey engine and charging the storage batteries was assigned to the ship's carpenter. So Benny acquired an extra title, coxswain.

X

We considered ourselves seamen, not yachtsmen. As seamen, we could land in any port in the world without passports. But someone raised the question. What if we could not make it to the race in 70 days?

"Then we would skip sailing up and down the American coasts and go through the Panama Canal," I said. "As soon as we reach America, we could have the junk shipped across the continent on land. That would take just three or four days."

"Shipping a 80-foot boat on land?"

"Believe me, Americans can move anything, including houses."

"How can we find such a ship shipper?"

"We'll ask that question when it becomes necessary."

"Wouldn't we need some kind of paper to travel on land then?" Reno raised the crucial question.

Yes, we would need passports.

When we went to apply for our passports, we were denied because we could not fit into any of the two categories of people the government allowed to leave: students studying abroad and officials on government business. Fortunately being a United Nations agency, which paid higher salaries than the Chinese government, FRA had a collection of people from all walks of life. One of the members on the FRA Board of Executives, Mr. Wang Shin-Heng, was a legislator. Within a week he got us our passports. In our passports we were classified as "Participants in International Yacht Race". Were we students or officials? What did we care?

Then we realized that passports alone would not permit us to travel in a foreign country. We would need visas.

So we went to Taipei to get our visas. We were met by a Chinese with a poker face in the American Consulate. After taking a quick look at our applications, he asked us to wait while he took them into an inner room. Barely a minute later, the door flung open and a neatly dressed American appeared in the doorway.

"Gao shen me gui?" in a pure Peking accent the American stunned us in Chinese. There was no one else in the office. So he must be speaking to us. What did we do wrong? We looked at each other and did not know what to say. Then he repeated in English in a nicer tone, "What is this? A yacht race?"

We could not tell whether that was ridicule or an expression of disbelief. Should we answer him in Chinese or in English? We nodded without uttering a word.

"You have a yacht?" his eyes swept our faces from one to another with a cynical look. Should we have put on better clothes to come to his office? It was too late. We acknowledged with more nodding,

"We have a junk."

"A junk in a yacht race?"

We nodded again.

"How are you going to get this junk of yours over there?"

"She sails."

"I'll be damned! Come on in." He led us into the inner office.

When we came out of the American vice consul's office an hour later, he introduced us to the poker face, "This is Mr. Yen. He will take care of the details."

The Queen of Spade suddenly changed into the face of the Joker. "Each of you need to deposit $500 under your own name in an American bank in America," he told us. "Come back to see me with your passport when you get a letter from the bank verifying your deposit."

I dashed out a letter to my uncle who was living in New York. I asked him if he could deposit $500 for each of us in a bank, which we promised to withdraw and return to him as soon as we landed in the United States. This was a common practice among all the Chinese students who applied for visas to the United States.

The Junk that Challenged the Yachts

One such $500 deposit could sometimes be passed on to guarantee ten or more students. I wondered if the American consul was aware of that. Later I was told that the purpose of requiring a deposit in an American bank was to ensure that the visitor would never become a social liability. Since no Chinese student had ever become an American social liability, I guessed it did not matter.

That Sunday we had a surprise visitor at the boatyard. It was the American vice consul who had interviewed us at the American Consulate. He introduced himself as Calvin Mehlert. "You can call me Cal," he said. From the clumsy way he walked on deck and the questions he asked we figured that he was a real landlubber. He stayed until we quit for the day.

"Let me give you a ride home," he offered. He had a jeep! We all piled in on it.

In all my life, I had never known anyone owning a car. Even the general manager and the chairman of the board of our Fishery Administration did not own cars. There were only company cars.

The vice consul spoke Chinese without any foreign accent. When he talked, even his hands moved like those of a Chinese. Out of politeness, we asked him to stay for dinner expecting him to decline according to the Chinese custom.

"I love Chinese food," our guest said. "My room mate and I have Chinese food everyday. I can eat rice all my life."

Then he went into a long soliloquy to introduce himself from his boyhood life to his first visit to China as an 18-year-old marine and later his study of the Chinese language at University of California and international relations at the School of Advanced International Studies at Georgetown University. Advanced studies? What could be more advanced than the college? That was way above our heads. Why did he tell us all that?

It became clear after dinner.

"I noticed on the day you came into my office for visas that there were six names with one crossed out. Today I noticed that there are six bunks on the junk. I wonder if you guys would consider to let me join."

"Join what?" all five of us asked in one voice.

"Join you, just getting across the Pacific, not the race. I know that the race is an all Chinese thing."

When he got no answer from us, he said, "You see, I am a San Franciscan. I have lots of relatives and friends there. I love to eat Chinese food. I can have Chinese food everyday."

Still seeing no response from us, he said, "Listen, it's getting late. I guess you guys have to go work on the junk early in the morning. I'll leave. But let's keep in touch."

As soon as the American left, Huloo asked us, "Did you guys hear him asking us to listen to him? He hasn't even joined us yet. We don't need a sixth crew, not to mention he's a foreigner. Can't you guys see that he has never been around boats? He's only going to be a pain in the ass."

"These Americans!" scoffed Reno. "Whenever they get their hands on something, they always become the heroes and get all the girls. Have you seen that movie, The World of Susie Wong? At the end, William Holden got Nancy Kwan."

"We don't have any Susie Wong or Nancy Kwan on board," I said.

"But we have those reporters on our tails. You know what? If he joins us, I bet those reporters will play him up as they played up a white climber of the Himalaya. We will all be his Sherpas."

"I hate Americans," Benny joined in. "Particularly those in uniforms who drive Jeeps."

"What does that have to do with driving Jeeps?" Marco asked.

"My brother was killed by a Jeep driven by one of those drunken American marines."

"Eh, that's just one drunken marine," said Reno. "Got nothing to do with this one."

"He drives a jeep. How do we know he could get along with us?"

"He can't drive his jeep on our junk, that's for sure, ha ha ha ha..." Marco was the only one who chuckled at his own joke. No one else did. "He seems to be a nice guy though." To Marco, everybody was a nice guy.

"Nice guy. We don't need nice guy. We need able seamen,"

Huloo said.

"I thought you said you could handle it all by yourself. What do you care about another able seaman?" I reminded him. That made him mad and ignited a heated argument between us. Huloo was dead against taking in any extra crew. I argued, with one delay after another, we would probably not have enough time to sail down to Panama Canal and then up the East Coast of America again. Very likely we would have to ship the junk on land. But none of us knew anything about transporting a boat on land. In fact, none of us, except myself, had ever heard of such thing. Having a native person on board would make things easier. Then everyone joined in. Benny was on Huloo's side, no foreigner. Reno agreed with me. A foreigner might come out handy. Marco did not take any side. He was trying to stop the argument.

After a while, Benny seemed to have second thought.

"This I must admit," he said. "His Chinese is better than mine. We can communicate with each other."

"Everybody speaks better Chinese than you do," said Reno. The two of them would grab on any chance to pick on each another. "The problem is his. Will he be able to understand your Cantonese accent?"

"Speak for yourself!"

"I am."

"Look, guys," I interrupted. "If we have to ship the junk across the American continent, how are we going to find a shipper? This guy is a San Franciscan."

"Only if he goes as a passenger," Huloo finally backed down. We all agreed. Then he added, "But I doubt if he will fit in."

"He said he could eat Chinese food everyday."

"Yeah, wait until he sees what Chinese grub means on shipboard."

Paul Chow

XI

The junk was finally ready to come off the slipway. If her former owner had seen her now, he would no doubt have doubled or tripled the price. Her body was painted yellow, her cabin done in white, her name in black and her bottom coated in copper-tone. All her youthful beauties, the bulging eyes, the flowery Eight Fairies Crossing the Sea on the bow and a pair of colorful phoenixes in a green background of seascape on the fantail, were brought vividly back to life. Even her brownish ragged sails were replaced by snow-white canvas. The work had taken 26 days.

On March 8, six months after I read about the yacht race in the paper and 95 days before the starting day of the race, the junk was launched. The boatyard staged a big launching celebration with firecrackers. We had asked the Governor's wife to christen her with her new name, *Free China,* that her husband had "bought". She could not come. So the mayor's wife came in her place. Cal brought a bottle of French Champaign. We tethered it to the bow in such a way that once released it would swing by its own weight and crash on the bow. But the mayor's wife wanted to help. She threw the bottle toward the junk. The bottle bobbed and was torn off the tether. It fell and broke. Watching the foam rising on the slipway, Marco turned to Calvin and said,

"See what I told you? What a waste. You should have let me drink it. I have never tasted Champaign before."

After the launching, we had the junk towed to the FRA dock. That evening, we slept in our new home, the *Free China.*

The next morning, with my savings of $850 in my pocket, I went to pay for the repair bill. To my great surprise, the manager of the boatyard, Fung Chuang, said to me, "There is no bill."

41

"What do you mean no bill?" I asked.

"No charge."

"Don't joke with me," I said.

"I'm not joking. It's a direct order from the Chairman."

I could not believe what I had just heard. Gen. Chen Liang was the chairman of the Board of Executives of FRA. Before coming to FRA, he served as the last mayor of Shanghai and, before that, he was the Commander of Quartermaster for the combined armed forces, Navy, Military and Air Force. I had had some squabble with him over the procurement of the engines for our steam trawlers that were being converted to diesel under my supervision. When my choice of engines was being overruled, I was so angry that I accused him behind his back of the corruption that I had read on a tabloid. When this got to his ears, he called me to his office. In front of all the heads of departments in FRA, he showed me a letter from the Vice President clearing him of the accusation after a thorough investigation. Then he told me that, under the Martial Law, those who spread rumors were punishable by death. After I admitted wrongdoing, the General turned to the department heads and said, "Nothing has taken place here. I don't want to hear another word about this." Since then I tried to avoid seeing the General face to face.

I went to the Chairman's office to thank him. It was the first time I saw him since our squabble. He asked me if there was anything else that he could do to help me. I reluctantly told him that we still did not have provisions for the trip and winter clothes for the North Pacific climate.

"Let me talk to the Commander-in-Chief of the Navy. I used to supply his entire Navy. Now it is his turn to support my boys," the General chuckled. He called us *his boys!* Did that include me? Then he continued, "I can also call Mr. Chiang Ching-Kuo and see what he can do. His father and I are close friends since our military school days."

Chiang Ching-Kuo's father was the President, Chiang Kai-Shek. At the time, the younger Chiang was the head of the Bureau of Politics for the armed forces. Within a week, both of them received us. The Commander-in-Chief of the Navy, Admiral Liang Hsu Chao, not only gave us winter clothes but also an advice.

"You should follow the rout of the explorations of the Ming Dynasty Eunuch Admiral Zheng He," the Admiral suggested. "That course will keep you close to shore most of the time. You will be able to get into port in case of an emergency."

"That was what we first thought of," I lied. How could I tell him that the crossing of the Pacific was more of a challenge to me than the yacht race? Knowing that I was abrasive, the General had warned me ahead of time not to be disagreeable when I talked to these high officials. "But our race is scheduled to start on June 11. This is already March. Going across the Pacific will be shorter."

"True. But have you taken your junk out to sea yet?"

"No."

"Crossing the Pacific is a lot of sailing for a shakedown cruise, you know," the Admiral's voice changed from being serious to being humorous.

"But there is no navigational hazard in the Pacific. Once we reach the American coast, the rest of the sailing will be along the coast. If there is going to be any work done on the junk, we can go into San Francisco."

"You do that!" said the Admiral.

The meeting with Gen. Chiang Ching-Kuo was very cordial and brief. He did not offer any advice or help. When we told him that we were still short of food supply for the trip, he only offered encouragement. He seemed to be more interested in having a picture taken with us. After the picture, he invited us to a dinner, which he did not attend. But he made sure that his secretary signed us up as members of his pet project, the Anti-Communist National Salvation Youth Corps.

Knowing that we were still looking for food, Cal, the American vice consul now a crewmember of the *Free China,* took me to see Gen. William Chase, the commander of the American Military Assistance Advisory Group (MAAG). Gen. Chase was the highest-ranking American military personnel in Taiwan. After listening to my plan on entering a junk into a yacht race and our need for provisions, the general gave us some commissary food. Then he turned to the Chinese liaison officer in his office and said, "This is what your country needs, more activities like this from the people rather than sending missions and high-ranking officials to Washington to ask for more aid. This is a golden chance for you to pitch some propaganda to the American people. These boys are the best ambassadors you can ever find for your country."

The liaison officer asked us to step into his office after we came out of the general's office. "I will assign a propaganda officer on your junk," he said. "I'll..."

"Wait a minute. That is not what the general said," Cal interrupted the liaison officer. I was so glad that Cal was with me. I would not know how to handle the situation nor have the audacity to talk to a military official like that. "What the general said is that these young men are the best propaganda the Chinese people can send. Putting an officer on board would be exactly what the general is opposing to. Didn't you hear the General criticizing your government in sending missions and high-ranking officials to Washington? He said these boys are the best ambassadors you can ever find for your country."

The liaison officer was speechless for a while. Then he said, "Come with me. I'll take you to the commissary." At the commissary, they loaded Cal's jeep up with boxes of canned food. They were mostly fruits and soup, no staple food.

We still needed to get real food for our trip, such as rice and flour. We could buy them. But that would take a big chunk of my savings. How would the six of us expect to live half a globe away from home after the race? I asked Mrs. Hunter, a missionary lady who was my former English teacher, to give me some idea. She knew many important people such as Mme. Chiang Kai-Shek and Gen. Chase.

A few days later I got a message from Mrs. Hunter telling me to go to a luncheon meeting at the Taipei Rotary Club on the following day.

I told her that I was seeking a six-month food supply for six people, not a lunch."

"Go," she said. "They want to hear your story. How often do people hear about an ancient Chinese junk sailing across oceans? It's a free lunch. You've got nothing to lose."

I went. After I finished my talk, a lot of questions were raised from the floor.

"What theory are you trying to prove?" someone asked.

Was I supposed to prove some theory? I had never thought of that. I had to make up some answer on the spot.

"That junks could sail better than the yachts?" I was not quite sure of what I said.

"I don't mean that," the inquirer clarified. "I mean a theory like the earth is round or the ocean current is flowing from west to east or the first American native people were from China."

I was stricken dumb and speechless. The audience suddenly became very quiet, waiting for my answer. I knew I had to say something. So I said,

"I guess the earth is round."

That brought a loud laughter. Then another question followed, "When are you planning to leave?"

I did not even know that myself. In embarrassment, I told them that depended on when we could find a way to get the provisions.

"How much would you need?" the president of the club asked.

"Enough for six people for six months," I said.

"Why don't you go home and figure out what you need and then let me know."

I pulled out from my pocket a list that we had compiled in the previous evening, "I have it right here."

That brought a loud roaring from the audience. As the president was reading the list, I pulled out a stack of carbon copies and distributed them among the audience. A big applause accompanied by foot-stamping, table-pounding and catcalls rose to fill the room. I was confused. I did not know what to make of it.

A week later, a truck and several black official cars pulled alongside the junk at the FRA dock. Men dressed in nice suits came out from the cars. Among them I could recognize Hsu Ren-Shou, the Harbor Master, Tang Tong-Sun, the Chief Pilot, Mr. Sun, the Mayor's secretary, Chi Shi, the Chief Engineer of Taiwan Shipbuilding Company, Wu Guan-Hsiung, the Deputy Manager of FRA, the American minister of the only protestant church in Keelung and the dentist who had pulled out my dead tooth that was murdered by Huloo at sea. Before we realized what was going on, these men peeled off their coats and rolled up their sleeves and started to move bags and cases from the truck to the junk. There were 500 lbs of rice, 20 lbs of peanuts, 20 lbs of soybeans, 10 bags of flour, 12 dozens of canned meat, 1 1/2 dozens of soy sauce, 28 lbs of tea, 3 bottles of beer and a small library of novels, enough to last us more than five months. It took the Rotarians half an hour to unload everything from the truck onto our deck.

XII

March 23, 1955, 80 days to go before the start of the race.

We took the *Free China* out to the open sea for a shakedown cruise. It was the first time any of us had ever sailed on a sailboat. We watched in awe as the *laoda* maneuvered her skillfully in tacking and jibing with the wind coming in all directions.

Some journalists went along to report for their papers. They became seasick as soon as we got out of the breakwater. We put them in the cabin to get them out of our way. All they could see through the cabin door was the five of us shouting and running excitedly through a web of ropes among the masts and sails. From where they were, they could not see the *laoda* in control on the tiller. The following description appeared on all the newspapers in Taiwan.

"The five young ocean-bound sailors handled the *Free China* expertly like the old sea salts in a Hollywood Spanish Main movie."

When we got back to port three hours later and had the junk tied down along the FRA dock, we suddenly realized that none of us had ever put our hands on the tiller during the entire exercise. Benny insisted that we should take her out again to get more familiarized with the sails before setting sail.

"How much more familiarized?" Reno asked. The *laoda* left as soon as we returned from the shakedown cruise. "Eh, what's the difference between taking her out on more trial runs without an experienced junkman to advise us and trying to figure things out by ourselves at sea when we will have plenty of time?" Reno argued.

"You city boys will never learn about the sea," Benny scoffed sulkily.

By this time, the news on the *Free China* had moved to the front page of every newspaper in Taiwan. With this kind of publicity and the support of all the important people such as the Governor, the Mayor, the Harbor Master, the Head of the Red Cross, the Commander in Chief of the Navy, the Chief of the Department of Politics for the Armed Forces, the Commander of the American Military Advisory Group and the Rotary Club, the wheel of bureaucracy started to turn. We had received every necessary paper to set sail except the sailing permit and the sailing charts. The sailing permit depended on my passing of the radio operator's test and the charts depended on the overseas postal service.

The reporters continued to bombard us with interviews and picture taking. Some paper had announced a contest to guess our time and date of our arrival on the American Continent. They wanted to know our departure date.

The New York Yacht Club wanted to know if we wanted to make reservations for hotel and banquet in Gothenburg. It sounded so strange to us. All our lives we lived where we worked. When I was in the army, the barracks was my home. When we were fishing, fishing boats were our homes. Now we are on the junk. The junk was our home. Why would we need hotel reservations? I couldn't figure out what was going through these yachtsmen's heads. Abandoning their ships whenever they are in port? We were sure sailing into a different world.

The Post Office delivered a pouch for us to carry to the San Francisco Post Office. All the letters, we were told, were canceled with a special seal to commemorate our voyage. There was one more thing for us to worry about. In case of shipwreck, postal mails and ship's log were supposed to be treated with equal importance.

The Marine Product Research Institute delivered 300 glass bottles for us to test the ocean current. In each bottle there was a note asking the founder to send it back to the Institute. What did Marine Product have to do with ocean current?

The Anti-Communist National Salvation Youth Corps officials wanted to recruit us as members. Luckily we had a spokesman, our captain Marco. His job was to shield them off from us. He did but he ended up in being forced to sign on as a member of the Youth Corps.

One day a white launch flying an American flag pulled alongside us. One of the two sailors in white uniforms standing on deck sang out in English: "Request permission for boarding!"

As I was trying to figure out whether it was a question or a demand, an officer came out of the cabin and hopped on board. He introduced himself as Capt. Chase, the Captain of the American Seaplane Tender, USS Pine Island. He said he had always been interested in Chinese junks but had never had a chance to get on board one.

"Can I take a look at your Number One Hold?" he asked.

What a strange request! I could not understand. Anyway, I took him to the bow and opened the hatch. He shook his head and pointed to the one forward of it. "That one," he said. I opened it and he climbed in. I heard him exclaimed, "I'll be damned!" I jumped down to see what was wrong. He pointed to the bottom and said to me, "See those two holes?"

"Yes, we will have them plugged up before we sail," I said apologetically. "We just didn't have time to get around doing it."

"Don't do that!" warned the American captain. "They were put there for a purpose."

"Did you say purpose?"

"Yes, they are shock absorbers so to speak. All the Chinese junks have them. When the boat dips her bow in a pitch, water is shipped in through those holes. The stored water then acts as a ballast to slow down the lifting of the bow. By the time the bow reaches its maximum height, the water will have all leaked out."

"I'll be damned," I imitated the American captain's exclamation.

"There are more innovative features in Chinese junks that the western boats do not have," the captain continued. "For instance, there is no shroud on your masts. Can I take a look at the base of your mainmast?"

I opened the hold next to the mainmast and showed him the nail-less support of its base against the bulkhead and the two side wedge-boards.

"See those boards?" the American captain pointed to the bulkheads and asked. "How many of them do you have?"

"Ten, not counting the bow stem and the stern transom."

"Amazing! They are all watertight."

"Watertight?"

"Yes, so that if there were a leak in one compartment the water would be confined locally and not leaked to the other compartments. This makes the junks unsinkable. Can you imagine that the junks have had them for thousands of years and we only have them now on the submarines."

"I'll be damned," was the only words I could find to say. I could understand why did the submarines have watertight bulkheads. They were made of steel. But I could not understand why the junks would have them. They were made of wood. Wood floats.

The American took us back to his ship and gave us a lifeboat compass and a box of distress rockets and a pistol launcher. With Fung Chuang's battery-operated signal light, we were well prepared for shipwreck.

The head of Western Enterprise, Capt. Barkus, also paid us a visit. He sounded like an expert of junks. "Where is your life boat?" was the first thing he asked.

Western Enterprise had a dock and a slipway not too far from the FRA dock. Everyone on the waterfront knew that it was the cover for the American secret operation sponsored by its Central Intelligence Agency. It carried out routine secret missions on the China coast in armored motorized junks. In response to Capt. Barkus's question, we showed him our leaky sampan.

"That thing?" the Australian captain shook his head in surprise. Then he left without saying a word. Half an hour later, he returned with a huge black package. He unfolded it on our deck and started to pump it up. A few minutes later, a good size rubber raft appeared in front of our eyes.

"This will take any weather," he said. "That sampan of yours won't last a minute."

We prayed we would never use it.

I took the radio operator's test and came short of the required speed to pass it. After Mr. Lai, the director of the FRA Radio Station, pleaded with the examiner by telling them that he had made special arrangements with some Japanese and American stations not to treat me as a professional operator but as an amateur, I received my license.

Mr. Lai seemed to be more excited than me.

"Here is your station identification," he said. "BEDM. Write it down. You should use it to identify yourself every time you get on the air. And here are the radio stations that I have arranged for you to contact at sea." He handed me a list.

GMT	STATION	FREQ. (KC)
0000-0015	NPG SAN FRANCISCO	5545, 9455
0055-0130	VPS HONG KONG	8566
0255-0300	NPG SAN FRANCISCO	5545, 9455
0320-0340	JMC TOKYO	8.5 MC
0355-0415	NPM HONOLULU	4802.5, 9440
0700-0715	KPH SAN PEDRO	8.7 MC
0755-0800	CQ CQ CQ	8364
0800-0805	NPG SAN FRANCISCO	5545, 9455
0920-0940	JMC TOKYO	8.5 MC
1130-1150	VPS HONG KONG	8566
1155-1200	CQ CQ CQ	8364
1200-1215	NPG SAN FRANCISCO	5545, 9455
1530-1545	NPM HONOLULU	4802.5, 9440
1620-1640	KTK SAN FRANCISCO	8687
1655-1700	NPG SAN FRANCISCO	5545, 9455
2130-2145	NPM HONOLULU	4802.5, 9440
2120-2150	JMC TOKYO	8.5 MC
2155-2200	CQ CQ CQ	8364
2355-2400	NPG SAN FRANCISCO	5545, 9455

"It covers 24 hours!" I said in disbelief.

"Yes," said Mr. Lai who seemed to be proud of his efforts. "Isn't it nice? Every hour is covered."

"When am I supposed to sleep?"

"Oh, I'm not asking you to call on every hour. All I want you to do is to call CQ (meaning all vessels at sea) three times a day, one in the morning, one at noon and one in the evening. At close range, you can call us. Our call sign is XSX at frequency 8714 kc. But we cannot reach very far. You will very soon get out of our range. Then you can call any of them. I suggest you call a fixed station at a fixed time so that the operator on the other side can get to know you."

With my radio operator's license, we got the last piece of document to clear us for our departure – the sailing permit. As far as we were concerned, the radio had no other purpose but to get the sailing permit. Once we were out in the ocean and thousands of miles from shore, what could a radio do? Would it bring us a fair wind?

What we were really short of was the sailing charts. Cap had sent a set to me from California. But till this day, we still had not received it. Fortunately, unlike Columbus, who had to answer the Spanish court whether he had any document to back him up, no one asked us about the sailing charts. I thought I would wait for two more days. By then if they still did not come, we would sail without them. After all, no junk sailor had ever seen a chart in his life. The Pacific Ocean was so wide and so deep, not as tricky as the Caribbean Sea to Columbus where there were so many uncharted underwater reefs and islands.

I went out and bought a world map for schools. With a sexton, a chronometer, a copy of mathematical tables, a copy of nautical almanac and a sky full of stars, I was as ready as Columbus or his predecessor, the Ming Dynasty Eunuch Admiral Zheng He (1405-1431).

XIII

March 30, 1955, 73 days to be counted down to the race.

The charts finally arrived this morning. I immediately spread them out on my chart table. Exactly as shown on the school map, there was no navigational hazard whatsoever in the Pacific Ocean. I could have easily sailed across the Pacific without them. On the weather charts I found the prevailing wind in the 43rd parallel. Again I could have sailed without them. Cap had told me where to find the wind.

I laid an easterly course to get out to the Pacific Ocean and then a NE/E course to the 43rd parallel. From there we would sail East again until we reached the American coast. I did not draw any more courses because I figured, as Cap said, once we made landfall on the American coast we could just follow the coastline and sail by landmarks. There were plenty of navigation lights marked on the chart.

I made the announcement of our departure date: April 4, 1955.

April 4, 1955

68 days before the start of the race.

The daily auction was long over and the cement floor was scrubbed clean when we were towed to the Fish Market dock for departure preparation this morning. We hung up all the flags we could find on board, the Blue-white-Red national flag, the golden dragon flag some friends made for us and the entire set of signal flags. There was a crowd gathered at the market. Among them we spotted some of our friends and colleagues. When we invited them aboard, the rest of the crowd followed. How could we refuse these curious people? People in Taiwan had rarely seen sailing vessels before. Once on deck, the thing that attracted them the most was not the boat. It was Huloo's two chickens. "Why are you having chickens on board?" they all asked.

"Tradition," Huloo told them "All junks carry chicken for eggs and pigs for garbage and, when time comes, for the sacrifice for teeth."

Lin Feng-Chu, our dropout crewmember, came with a full basket of pork lard.

"We can't use that much for cooking!" we said.

"It's not for you," Lin said. "It's for the masts."

"What does pork lard have to do with masts?"

"To slush the mast. The junk fishermen told me that the petroleum grease you put on your masts would cake up when exposed to seawater and would stop being lubricant. They said pork lard wouldn't cake up."

On the dock there was a podium. It was decorated with white tablecloth, fresh flowers, flags, loud speakers and overhead banners and firecrackers in bright wedding red. We were ushered ashore. The Chairman and Director of our fishing company were there. The mayor and the head of the Anti-Communist National Salvation Youth Corps were also there. We were showered with speeches, hand shaking, flower presenting and backslapping.

Then we returned to our boat. I found two girls sitting on my bunk. "What are you doing here, Miss. Lan?" I asked in great surprise. Miss. Lan had been taking English lessons from me in the evenings. Our lessons were interrupted when I received the telegram from the Racing Committee.

I had first noticed Miss Lan on the night train from Taipei to Keelung. She was tall and different from other girls I saw in Taiwan, both in her dress and her short hairstyle. She was Japanese mannered and shy with a smile on her face. She was speaking Japanese to her friend. Out of curiosity I asked her if they were Japanese. She said she was as Taiwanese as the water I drank. I saw her again several days later on the same night train when I was returning from Taipei with my Russian friend Boris Sarapouloff. She came over and asked if she could take English lesson from me so that she could save time in going to Taipei every evening after work.

"How do you know I am qualified?" I asked.

"You spoke fluently with that foreigner."

How could I refuse such a compliment from a pretty girl?

"We want to sail with you," said Miss. Lan, while remain sitting on my bunk.

I was stunned speechless.

"We can cook for you."

Why hadn't I thought of her when we were looking for a sixth crewmember?

"But..." I tried to search for some nice words to refuse her.

"You don't need to have much space to put us up. We are thin. We can easily fit into one bunk. Look," she said. Then she raised her handbag and continued, "My toiletry and clothes for change are all packed in here."

"You don't have the exit papers," I finally found a reason.

"We can hide. We have been down in the holds when you were ashore. There are so many cracks and holes where we can hide. I was told that seamen do not need passports to go into foreign ports."

"You will need visas."

56

"Don't you have an American visa consul on board?"

Just then the Joint Inspection Team of Customs/Police/Garrison came on board. They chased all the visitors ashore, including Marco's sister and her family and the two girls. As I watched her friend stooping under the low transom of the cabin door on her way out, I felt some soft hair brushing my eyes and wet lips touching my cheek. Then I smelled the familiar smell of the perfume Miss Lan wore every night when she came to our apartment for her lessons. But this was the first time we touched. That was very un-Chinese-like, bad Japanese mannered and embarrassing for me. Luckily there was no one in the cabin. Where did she learn to be so bold? Did she meet some American sailors?

A towline was secured on the base of our foremast. As we cast off our mooring lines, the firecrackers suddenly burst open and cracked out aloud over our heads. The confetti filled the space. The smoke sent tears to my eyes. They blurred my view of the dock and the people standing there waving their hands. I went into the cabin and climbed onto the rice sacks in the Navigation/Radio-corner. Bending over the chart table I made the first entry in our brand new logbook:

April 4, 1955
1300 LCT   Depart Fish Market in tow by M/V Minnesota,
courtesy of Capt. Chang Chang-Hai.

A tugboat loaded with people on both her deck and topside escorted us all the way out to the breakwater.

I could see our Chairman's shiny baldhead sticking out a head taller than the people around him on the bridge. He kept waving to us until we lost sight of them as we headed out to the open sea. Bless that old man! Without his support, we wouldn't be able to pass these breakwaters now. Without his big heart, I wouldn't be sailing with my junk mates. Instead, I would be sitting in jail on the Infernal Island if I had not already been executed by a firing squad.

The second entry in the logbook was:
1350 LCT   Part tow 5 miles outside of Keelung Breakwater.

The Junk that Challenged the Yachts

M/V Minnesota heads out to Fishing Zone 210

I had barely scratched in the last letter when I heard the low bass voice of our captain, Marco, roaring out on deck,

"Raise sails!"

I rushed back on deck.

There standing on the foot-thwart behind the cabin was Marco, with one hand on the tiller and one hand waving in the air like a true *laoda*. Huloo was forward by the foremast. Reno was on the poop deck holding the main sheets in his hand. Benny, dressed like a Portuguese fisherman in turtleneck sweater, leather boots, white cotton gloves and a navy blue flannel tam tilted on his head, was pulling up the main halyard on the winch drum that was driven by the 5 HP Danish engine given to us by M. Lin. Calvin was cooped up high on the last thwart on the fantail with his 16-mm motion picture camera.

The bundle that consisted of all 16 large bamboo poles, a wooden yard and 1800 square feet of wet canvas, which had been sitting on top of the cabin since the shake-up cruise eight days ago, lifted up slowly from its cradle. Just then a wave sneaked under the junk. The bundle, which weighed at least a ton, responded to the wave and swept across the top of the cabin. Reno tried to hold on to the sheets. But the swaying mass kept on going, dragging Reno along and knocking down everything that was in its way.

"Boy, this is going to make Hollywood look pale!" Cal exclaimed excitedly while kept shooting his movie.

We eventually got the sail up. The cabin top had been swept clean except the six screws sticking up without the compass they were supposed to anchor down and a short stub of tubing where the kitchen chimney had used to be. The cradle for the furled sail was nowhere to be seen.

As soon as we started sailing, I discovered that when one depended on the wind for propelling one could not steer on a course. One must zigzag along the course. The next hour was spent in shouting and pulling while we tried to get the junk on a comfortable tack. Suddenly both our sails puffed up. Then the junk came alive. She listed her body gracefully as a racing bike rounding a sharp bend. The sea was rushing aft and climbing occasionally over the bulwark to wet the deck. She was sailing!

Benny and Calvin took the first watch. "Do I have to stand watch?" Calvin asked the captain in a tone which I could not make out whether he was joking or serious. I assumed it was American humor. "I thought I was a passenger."

"Yes, when we are in port," Marco said. "When we are at sea, there is no passenger. Everyone is an able junkman."

"But every junkman has a title. What is mine?"

"Ship's Photographer, since you have a motion picture camera. How does that sound?" Not just a camera, Cal had 2500 feet of Kodachrome film to go with it. Actually it was the other way around. He got the (expired) film first as a throw-away from the American military commissary and then went out to buy a camera to go with the film. After thinking a while, Marco added, "Wait a minute. I noticed that you never got involved in any of our arguments. You must be objective, the qualification of a historian. How about the ship's historian, ha, ha, ha, ha?"

I interrupted their conversation. "Let's steer NE," I said to the watch. "After we see the Agincourt Light, we will change course to East to get out to the Pacific."

"Isn't Agincourt a French name?" Cal asked.

"Yes," I said. "So is Formosa. Remember, China used to be a quasi-colony of many foreign countries, England, France, Germany, Portuguese, Russia and Japan. The charts we are using are American. They prefer the Anglicized names."

After giving the course, I went inside the cabin to make another entry in the logbook:

1430 LCT   Full sail raised on both Fore and Main.
Ship position: 25° 25' N, 121° 30' E
(5 nautical miles N of Keelung breakwater)
Wind between N/W and N/E, 3 BS
Overcast and rain, Visibility 5 miles
Course NE
First tack Starboard with heading NW/N
Estimated speed: 5 knots,

Estimated speed made good: 3 knots
Estimated leeway 1 knot
Estimated time on course: 5 hrs

Attention, Watch:

> ***Maintain course NE***
> ***Change tack at 1530***
> ***Alert Navigator on sighting of Agincourt Light***

I turned on the radio, which was preset on 8364 kc. The voice of the radio operator at the Fisheries Station was scratchy,

"... Calling BEDM, calling BEDM. This is XSX. Come in please."

We did not have voice on our marine radio. I could only respond in Morse codes. But Keelung kept on calling. They must not have heard me.

I gave a few poundings on the black box. It only made more scratchy noise. I kicked it. It squealed more. Then it dawned on me that we had no antenna. It had been knocked down when we were raising the sail. I went out and hoisted it up on the mainmast. But I still could not send out any message.

I suddenly realized that the antenna was leaning against the sail. Any current would have been drained off to the wet canvas. I tried to hang the antenna on the flag post. I still got no response. I gave up.

In a way I was glad to sever my last earthly bondage. The *Free China* finally set me free! There would be no more reporters, no more house search, no more slogan mimicking and no more fake smiling when I did not feel like smiling.

Being cooped up in the listed chart room I started to feel seasick. I went to lie down in my bunk. The feeling was strange. There was no vibration of a propeller to feel. There was no sound of the engine and no squeaking of the hull to hear, just the rippling sound of waves through the hull and the flapping of the sails through the cabin's opening to the deck.

The past seven months was like a dream to me. The only thing that was real was my wet bunk. I found an empty cup and some flowers lying on my wet blanket. But I was so sick that I could care less. I pulled the blanket over my head. I smelled Miss. Lan. That silly girl! I fell asleep.

The change of tack woke me up. I came on deck. It was pitch black. The sleep and the fresh air had taken away my seasickness. I noticed a light flashing on our starboard quarter.

"Are we at Agincourt already?" I asked. "Why didn't you guys wake me up?"

"That's Keelung Light," Benny pointed out to me. "Agincourt is still way out there."

I timed the flashes, took a bearing of it and read the dial on the patent log trolling on the fantail and then went into the cabin. I made another entry in the logbook:

2400 LCT   Full sail remain on both Fore and Main.
                    Maintaining course NE
                    On port tack making 4 knots
                    Estimated leeway 2 knot
                    Wind N 4 BC
                    Sky overcast and rain

When I came back on deck I felt hungry. I had not had anything to eat since breakfast.

"Who's turn to cook?" I asked.

"No dinner today," Benny said.

"What's going on?"

"The stove won't cook. Its candle light won't even warm a pot of water."

"Why not?"

"No chimney."

No dinner? No hot tea? It's going to be a long miserable night.

April 5, 1955

As the sky turned from pitch dark to grayish white like a bellied-up swordfish being slowly pulled out from the deep, the flashing of the light house vanished and the sky fused together with the sea into a primordial soup. When daylight was finally upon us, the water got separated from the firmament. To my shocking disappointment, the Keelung mountains popped out of the misty and drizzling southern horizon. They were so close that I could even make out some of the buildings on shore. If we could see them at sea, they should certainly be able to see us from shore. What would they think of us?

I took some bearings and plotted a fix on our position on the chart. It was so far off the position that was arrived by dead reckoning. The reason must be the frequent tacking each watch was making. The junk was making such slow speed that the rotor of the ship's log was hanging straight up and down and not turning. So the distances entered in the logbook were all rough estimates, plus the fact that I did not know how to estimate the leeway.

First thing first, we must get out of the sight of those shore people. Skipping Agincourt, I changed course to due East.

The new course put the wind directly on our port beam. We immediately picked up speed. The line on the ship's log stretched out and started to turn. It registered 6 knots. It was the first time we had ever seen the junk travel so fast. The speed left all the hard feeling, grumbling, doubts and impatience of the crew behind. Even Huloo's chickens joined us in the good mood. One of them clucked, announcing the delivery of the first egg of the voyage. It was Cal's turn to eat the egg. Unlike us, who would just poke two holes on its ends and suck out the content, he made a big production in frying it as we all watched. It took him half an hour on the tiny fire made by the dripping diesel and water. I suspected that he was intentionally putting on a show to entice us.

I tried once more to contact Keelung on the radio. Just like the day before, I could only hear them calling us but not responding to my answer. The antenna on the flagpole was not touching anything. Definitely it must be something wrong with my transmitter.

Dark clouds started to gather in the afternoon. The Keelung mountains disappeared over the horizon.

April 6, 1955

The rain returned after midnight. The wind got stronger. The junk was making 7 knots. We started to worry about the mast. Leaning heavily to the starboard side, it left a gap on its port side in its base.

The base consisted of two two-inch-thick boards. The mast was wedged between these boards while leaning against the aft bulkhead and shored by two sticks of inch-and-half diameter against the fore bulkhead. Besides these supports, there were no nails, no shrouds and no stays.

We decided to shorten the sail. At first, it wouldn't come down when we loosened the halyard. The sliding rings would not slide on the mast. Then we realized what Lin had told us. The petroleum grease must have been caked up by the saltwater. We should have slushed the mast with Pork lard. Too late, we could only pull on the downhaul. Suddenly the sail slid about three feet and stopped. No matter how hard we pulled on the downhaul, it would not slide any further. The halyard got stuck in the hoisting block.

We brought the junk into the wind immediately. Huloo, the sail master, got up on the sail by climbing from one bamboo batten to another until he reached the gaff. He found that the halyard was jammed in the block. There was no way to get it out. He asked that a 1/4" rope, a snatch block, a knife and a marlinspike be sent up to him.

After securing the snatch block, the gaff and himself to the mast with the 1/4", Huloo cut the halyard from the jammed block and spliced it back up again. Then he fed it into the snatch block.

"What took you so long?" we asked him when he got back on deck.

"Why don't you go try splicing that stiff rope on a swinging mast yourself," Huloo retorted. "Which *wang-ba-dan* ordered that *bi-yang-de* Taiwan sisal for halyard? For one thing, it is one size too small. When it gets wet, it is as hard as my *ji-ba* when it gets excited It was like a Pekingese trying to *cao* a Swiss St. Bernard. There is no way to prevent it from falling into the crack of the sheave."

The Junk that Challenged the Yachts

We looked for a spare block in the storage hold. We found all kinds of tools Benny had ordered but no spare block. Huloo tried to repair the broken one. By the end of the day, he gave up.

"We can't sail on like this," he told us. "We must return to Keelung."

That brought a long silence on deck.

Huloo reasoned that the single block he put on the mast had doubled or tripled the strain on the mast. It would widen the gap further at its base. "We also need to get some soft Manila for the halyard," he said. "The right size."

"Let's head back then," Benny said. "How many times have I told you guys that we were not ready?"

"Ordering the wrong rope has no *diao* thing to do with readiness," Reno commented. "Why don't you admit you *ta-ma-de* screwed it up?"

"*Gan-ni-nao,* why didn't you do the ordering then?" Benny raised his voice. His face was all red.

"None of you *wang-ba-dan* asked me. Let me tell you. If we returned, they would for sure get us by our *ji-ba*. That would be the end of our trip."

"If we lost our mast, you would not just lose your *ji-ba,* you would lose that bitch life of yours," Huloo warned.

"Perhaps we could put in to the next closest port," Marco suggested, "I'm sure they have ropes and blocks in Okinawa."

"The radio also needs to be fixed," Benny added.

"You mean that *lanjiao* Paul has been playing with? Its only useful for the newspapers to sell more papers," Reno said. "You think they would dispatch a rescue to us if we got stuck in the middle of the ocean?"

"We can return to Keelung and not go in," I suggested.

"*Ta-ma-de,* what kind of *gui-che-de* talk is that?"

"We could drop anchor inside the breakwater and do our repairs there. Without entering the port, we not only keep our sailing permit but also stay out of the authority and the reporters."

The argument went on all day. During that time, the junk kept heading out toward the open ocean. All through our discussions,

Cal listened in with an intense interest. I could not tell how much he had picked up from our salty talk.

After dinner we decided to take a vote. Yes for returning to Keelung had 4 votes, nay had 1 with one abstention.

We turned the boat around.

"We can consider this our shakedown cruise," Huloo tried to justify our decision.

"It sure shook us down," Marco said.

"It sunk us," Reno added bitterly.

The returning trip was much smoother. No more shouting on deck when we tacked. Whoever was at the tiller at the time of tacking now acted like a true *laoda*. The two and half day outbound sailing took just six hours for our return trip. At half way, we sighted the purse seiner MV Yu-Hsiang. Not having received any radio message from us since we left port two days ago, the Port Captain of the fishing fleet decided to send her out to look for us. We asked her to relay a message to inform the office of our return. At 2130 LCT (local civil time), we dropped our anchor inside the breakwater of Keelung harbor. The deck was leveled for the first time in three days. We all had a good sleep.

April 7, 1955

A launch pulled alongside our junk early in the morning. It carried the inspectors of the Joint Inspection Team of Customs/Police/Garrison. We told them we did not want to clear customs. But they said they had an order to bring us in.

As soon as we tied down our junk, we were served with an order to abort our trip. The sailing permit was pulled away from us. There went my dream and all the work I had put in during the past five months. I heard Reno mumbling in disgust,

"See what I told you?"

XIV

All day long we were swarmed by reporters and friends. Nothing could be more humiliating for us to face them and to be bombarded by their silly questions.

Marco's sister scolded me for not trying hard enough to maintain radio contact with our home office FRA.

"It worried me to death," she said to me. "I could not eat or sit or close my eyes for all those days."

All we had to do to avoid further embarrassment was to fix the radio, rig up a new halyard and get the hell out of this place. It would take just a few hours. But without a sailing permit, we would not even be able to make it to the breakwater.

We did not know what to do. We figured the only person who could possibly bail us out was the General, the chairman of the board at FRA. He had been very supportive to us before.

Although long retired from military before coming to FRA, Gen. Chen Liang was still a very influential figure in the military and politics arena in Taiwan. The President, Chiang Kai-Shek, was his schoolmate. Many military heads including the head of the Garrison Command, Peng Meng-Ji, had either served under him or owed him big favors when he was in charge of supplying all the armed forces in China. We called on him.

Like everyone else, the General tried to persuade us to give up our trip.

"Forget about the yacht race. It's just a game for the Westerners," he said to us. "We have serious business to do at home. The company has determined to develop long-line fishing in the Indian Ocean. Why? You know it better than I do. But our boats are not big enough to go to Indian Ocean. So we have ordered from Japan several large long-distance fishing boats. Sailing the big oceans? There you are. If you boys are interested to join this project, I can send you to Japan right away. You will go on the Japanese boats to learn how they fish. When these boats are ready, you will each bring one back. Mark my words, long-lining is going to be the future of China's fishing industry. Don't you want to plan for your future?"

Seeing that our spokesman, Marco, remained silent, I spoke out. I thanked him for his advice and offer. Then I said, "At this time we cannot think about our future beyond this trip."

The General did not show any sign of surprise to my answer. He remained silent for a long time. Then he turned to the others and said, "You must each make your own decision independently. Don't let any of your shipmates talk you into doing something that you are going to regret for the rest of your life."

He cast a quick look at me. Then he asked them one by one what they wanted to do. The answers he got were the same as mine.

"You must realize what you are getting into," the General warned. "Once you get out there on the ocean, you are on your own. No one is going to go to your rescue if you get into any kind of trouble."

We told the General we understood that very well.

"Then there is only one way," he said in the voice of a field commander addressing his troop before a battle. "We must all work together with just one goal in mind: to get the junk out to sea. You go back and prepare the boat in the best way you know how. I'll take care of the bureaucracy of getting a sailing permit for you. But you had better not return this time because I won't help you to get another one."

We worked all day on the following day. We had our radio repaired. In addition, the official who was in charge of the radio communication of all the fishing boats in Taiwan, Lo Cheng-San, gave us an extra set of transmitter, TCS-13 exactly as the one I had, to use as a spare. We not only rigged a new halyard but also stocked up some spare blocks and Manila ropes. We mended the holes on the sail that were chafed out by the bamboo batten rubbing on the mast. We got more bamboo poles as spares, enough to make another set of battens. We slushed both masts with pork lard. We installed a new portable chimney for the cooking range. We dried our beddings and tidied the cabin.

While we were checking the holds, we discovered that the water in our new water tanks had all turned into a deep red color. Cheap lumber! Perhaps they needed pre-soaking. We drained the spoiled water out and filled the tanks back up with fresh water after a good flushing. By the end of the day, we had the junk shipshape for sea again.

On the next day, I was called to testify before an ad hoc committee that was to look into the fitness of the junk and her crew. Their recommendation would be forwarded to the highest authorities that were in charge of security and transportation. I had no idea who had ordered this investigation.

I found myself sitting nervously in a stiff posture and facing a group of old retired sea captains. Before asking me to tell them what had happened on our last voyage and why did we return to port, they started by telling me their own sea stories of the North Pacific in winter seasons, one more horrified than the other.

At the end of two long hours, the chairman, Capt. Yeh Shi-hsiang, said to me, "Do you have anything to add?"

To add? What could I add? Their stories were more colorful than mine. (They must have had a good time in getting someone to listen to their stories.) Suddenly I thought of the General's advice. I said, "I have learned a lot from listening to your valuable experiences." Then, sitting on the edge of my chair, I waited for the interrogation to begin.

It never came. I heard Capt. Yeh saying to me, "That's all. You may go."

The following few days were the longest days in our lives. No one talked. We just lay in our bunks listening to the old rubber tires squeaking between the boat and the dock and the ship's clock ticking away as we waited for the sailing permit.

April 15, 1955

We finally received our sailing permit. I was told that after the committee had certified the seaworthiness of the junk and the qualification of the crew, (Certified?) someone in the Prince's (Chiang Ching-Kuo) Bureau of Politics raised the question on our loyalty to the Republic.

"Without any exception, all those going abroad are required to have their parents and wives remain in Taiwan until they return. But none of these men has any relative in Taiwan. They are all from the Mainland. Their families are still there. What if they defect to the Communist? Who is going to be held responsible?"

When this question reached the ears of Gen. Chen Liang, he went directly to young Chiang and the Garrison Commander and told them that he would personally vouch for us.

XV

April 16, 1955

56 days to the starting of the race

We had not seen our American passenger since returning from our brief ill-fated voyage. Our clumsy performance at sea must have scared him away. We were surprised when we saw Cal show up on board this morning. "When are we pulling out?" he asked in a bobbling spirit. So there was someone else besides the General who had confidence in us.

"Have you ever had second thought in trusting your life to us?" we asked him.

"Why should I?" he said without thinking. "There are five of you and only one of me."

Did he refer YOU as Chinese and ME as American?

"This American marine is sure different from the rest of them," Benny made the comment after Cal went back on shore to say goodbye to his friends. "The ones I've seen before all thought that one American life was worth at least a hundred Chinese lives. This one is satisfied with five."

There were no flowers, no firecrackers and no crowds this time. The only streamers were heads poking out of the windows of the FRA building as we were being pulled away from the dock by the fishing boat, MV Yu-Hsiang. (Embarrassingly, we still did not have any confidence in maneuvering the junk in narrow waters.) Some friends of Cal's and Marco's came out on a tugboat, which accompanied us all the way to the breakwater. Sticking up above all the heads was the General's baldhead again.

On our way toward the breakwater, a fireboat appeared from nowhere. When she came to within a hundred meter from us, she suddenly opened up like a peacock showing off its feathers. Columns of torrents shot up, forming a beautiful white bouquet.

At the breakwater, an incoming Navy submarine chaser sounded out a string of rapid blasts that I often saw in the movies before they dropped their deep charges.

As we passed the entrance lights, a motorized junk overtook us. Her crew, a mixture of Chinese and Westerners, waved at us. She must be one of those Western Enterprise boats on her way to a secret mission on the Mainland coast.

Once outside of the breakwater, we parted tow and raised sails. We did it so expertly this time that not a single shout was heard on deck.

The sea breeze smelled so sweet and free. I felt great to shake off all my land dust and to cut loose all my shore bondages. I took a last look at the breakwater. I sure hoped I would never see those rocks again.

There was a condition attached to the issuing of our sailing permit this time. We must be subjected to an onboard assessment by a team of experts. Our tow was ordered to follow us. She would force us back if we failed the test. She would transport the experts back if we passed. The team was headed by an official from the FRA office, Mr. Chang Lei-Yu, and consisted of a fisherman, *Lao* Tseng I-Chuan, who had spent many years on junks before signing up the FRA boats, and a technician from the FRA radio station, *Hsiao* Huang Yen. (We fishermen addressed all those from the office with either *Mr.* or *Miss,* out of respect, old shipmates with *Lao,* meaning old, and people of our equal with *Hsiao,* meaning small or young.)

Marco, Reno and I yielded our bunks to the experts. Marco spread out his Navy coat on the rice sacks and claimed my radio/navigation corner to be the captain's "sea cabin". Reno and I figured that we could just climb into any bunks that would be vacated by those on watch.

We were sailing along pretty well until dusk. The wind died with the setting sun. The junk swung around and positioned her body athwart to the direction of the rolling waves. The 1800 square feet of rain-soaked canvas hanging on the mainmast and its eight heavy battens, each made up of two 4-inch bamboo poles, started swinging, shaking loose everything on board.

We could either rig up a sea-anchor, which most likely would not work when there was no wind, or ask for a tow from our escort, which, having also heaved to, was subjected to the same torture we were having. We decided on the latter. We certainly did not want to repeat what we did last time, being adrift in the same position in full view of the people on shore on the next morning.

April 17, 1955

We had been in tow all night. When we were under sail, the sails acted as stabilizers. The rolling was mild. All we could hear was the rushing water hitting the planking and the wake stirred up by the rudder. Now being under tow, she rolled like a drunken sailor. She moaned, squeaked and rattled. Among all these noises, there was a mysterious sound that we could not figure out. It was a rumbling sound that seemed to be coming from the bottoms of the holds.

At dawn, the wind started to pick up with the rising sun. We parted tow and raised our sails. It was good sailing. The rattling of the battens disappeared. So did the rumbling sound from the holds. We challenge our friends on the diesel boat for a race. As we were nudging ahead to the ballad of the ocean, a loud popping sound as that from the firing of a rifle suddenly tore through the air. Before we could figure out what it was, there came another one, then another one... The sheets jerked and slacked. My eyes followed them to the mainsail. The lower four battens were limping like the broken legs of a slaughtered chicken!

The helmsman quickly pushed the tiller down wind. The junk responded by swinging her bow into the wind and came to a standstill. We doused the mainsail. When it was lowered to a couple of feet short of reaching the cradle, the huge bundle of wet canvas and battens started to swing with the rolling motion of the junk. Benny hurriedly dumped the entire load on top of the cabin as Marco and Cal threw their bodies down to catch the wild beast.

Luckily nothing went overboard. We hailed the Yu Hsiang for a tow.

No Man Island was nearby. Our tow found a shielded cove and dropped her anchor. We did not drop ours. Our anchor hawser was made of split bamboo. It was mounted on a hand-cranked Spanish-windlass. Once released, it would take a lot of sweat and time to crank it back on the windlass again. Now we realized why the *laoda* said that it needed a crew of fourteen to handle the junk. We kept our tow on a shortened towline.

No Man Island is 90 nautical miles E/N off the northeast tip of Taiwan. It is referred to in the Chinese history book as Diao Yu Tai (The Fishing Platform). On the Japanese chart it is referred to as Sento Shosho.

No Man Island is one of the islands that form the Greater Taiwan Province, which consists of the main island, Taiwan, and many smaller islands around it. They are the Penghu Chain (Pascadors) to the southwest, Lanyu and Lutao (formerly known as Inferno Islet for detaining political prisoners) to the southeast, Guishan (Turtle Mountain), Guiluan (Turtle Egg), Woo-jen-tao (No Man Island) with its satellites, North Islet and South Islet, to the northeast and Peng-Chia Yu (Agincourt), Huaping Yu (Flowerpot) and Mianhua Yu (Cotton) to the north. Since the Ching Dynasty, even during the Japanese occupation of Taiwan, No Man Island has been under the administration of Yilan County. Because of its smallness in size and large distance from Japan, Japan did not include it in her annexation demand of the Ryukyu Chain (Okinawa) from China in the 1874 Treaty of Peking. But to the Taiwanese fishermen from Keelung and Su-Ao, it has been a shelter ever since their ancestors first went to sea.

It was still early. We started to work on the battens right away.

"We should have had them made evenly at both ends," Huloo said. That immediately started an argument.

Each batten was made of two bamboo poles of 4" diameter tied together. Near the leech (the outer edge of the sail) where we had assumed they would sustain little pressure, we used a single pole. That was where the trouble was. If we had given it a little thought, we should have realized that, since each batten was tied to a sheet, the force at the leech should be equal to that at the luff (the edge closest to the mast).

"It is like two men carrying a load on a pole," Huloo explained. "The loads on both men are equal."

Then the argument shifted to the position of the load. After some more arguments, everyone finally agreed with Huloo. On a sail, the load should be evenly distributed.

Once the argument was settled, it took us no time to make the new battens. Before sunset, we had all the eight 36-feet-long battens strengthened to three-pole evenly from end to end. Three formed a triangle that would sustain force in any direction.

The junk expert, *Lao* Tseng, was impressed with the way we arrived at our decision and at the speed we worked. He said he had never encountered such a problem when he was fishing on junks. Even if the problem did arise, it would have been the *laoda's* decision to make. "The crew would have no say." We told him this was called *Democracy.* Then he turned to our American crewmember and asked, "Is that how you people run your country?"

But in the eyes of Mr. Chang, we were just a bunch of rebel rousers with no leader. He was so amazed that we could get our problems solved. "I thought you had ironed out everything before coming out this time," he said to us. "Admit it, you are really inexperienced in junk sailing. Who knows what other unknown problems may pop up later. Take my advice. Return to Keelung and get every detail ironed out before you take her out to the open ocean again."

Although graduated from a marine product school, Mr. Chang had never spent a single day at sea. He was an office rat. What do office rats know about boats? But here he was the chef-de-mission. He would call the shot to our future. What could we do?

The Chinese believed in the Kitchen God, who resided in every kitchen throughout the whole year. He saw everything that took place in the family during the year. On the 23rd of the last month of each year, the Kitchen God would go back to Heaven to make his annual report to the Jade-Emperor God. It was a tradition for every family to give him a big send-off feast on that day. In truthfulness, the purpose of the feast was to get him drunk and to seal off his mouth so that he would not say anything bad about the family to the Jade-Emperor God. That was why wine and sticky-rice-cake were served. We thought we should pay the same respect to our experts, particularly Mr. Chang.

Huloo was the cook of the day. The crew on the Yu Hsiang brought over a bundle of bottles of rice wine tied with a straw string and a basket of flying fish that they had collected on their deck during the previous night. (They had their deck light on all night while towing us so that we could see the towline. That attracted the flying fish.) So we had "flied" (fried) flying fish as the main dish, fried peanuts as the appetizer, boiled (dehydrated) vegetable (thanks to the Joint Commission on Rural Reconstruction) as a side dish, beef noodles (handmade from flour and cans, thanks to the Rotary Club) as our main staple and (canned) peaches (thanks to Gen. Chase at MAAG) as dessert. Thank Heaven, we found some sweet rice among our provisions. We served sweet stick-rice-cake as the last course. With the crew of the Yu Hsiang joining us, we ate on the foredeck. Everyone had a good time, especially Marco. But the next morning, he received a harsh criticism from our moralist, Benny, and a stern lecture from the most senior member of the crew, Huloo. "What kind of seaman are you?" Huloo asked him. "No drinking at sea is traditionally obeyed by every seaman, let alone you being the captain and your getting drunk."

But most importantly, we got the experts merrily drunk.

XVI

April 18, 1955

The stop at No Man Island turned out to be a good move. Benny found that the rotary bilge pump that was driven by our 5-HP diesel engine had not been pumping. He took it apart and found that the brass rotor was all worn out. In just a couple of weeks? The chamber of the pump was filled with a smooth paste of sand and fibers. He also found that the entire bilge was filled with that stuff.

"We must replace the rotor," said Benny.

"With what?" asked Huloo.

"I'm sure Mr. Lin in Keelung must have spares for this engine. He has sold thousands of them to the farmers to pump water out of their rice paddies."

"You mean to go back to Keelung to look for this Mr. Lin?" asked Reno in rage. "Not over my dead body!"

"But the bilge must be pumped out. This is just the beginning. We have a long way to go yet."

"Look, if the bilge is filled with this stuff as you said," Huloo tried to calm the two with reasoning. "The new rotor will be ground out again in no time. We must find out where this smut comes from."

Then someone mentioned the rumbling sound from the bottoms of the holds. When we put two and two together, we concluded that there could be only one explanation. The sand, the fibers and the rumbling sound must all be generated by the same thing. The cobblestones! They were dumped in there as ballast without anything to hold them down. So they were free to roll and chafe on the bottom. The fibers were those chased off from the planking and the sand was that from the rocks. We must get them out before they chewed a hole in our bottom. But there were 5 tons of them!

To get to the rocks, we must first hoist all the empty oil drums out. There were 50 of them. We did not have enough space on deck to put them. Were we glad to see that Cal and *Hsiao* Huang had gone ashore to explore the island! At lease two out of four idling hands would be out of our way so that we could have more room to work.

The rocks in the empty holds could be reached easily. But those in the two holds where the four new water tanks were located were hard to get to. The tanks were fitted so snugly in the holds that there was hardly any room for a person to move around. Moreover, the space between the flat bottom of the tanks and the curved hull was only one foot high at the widest part.

"Only Hsiao Chow is small enough to get under it," said Marco. The crew had added an adjective, *Hsiao,* to Cal's and my names. *Hsiao* meant small in stature. "Besides, it was your big idea to use the rocks as ballast and to build the extra water tanks as reserve."

What could I say? I stripped naked and greased my body so that I could squeeze underneath the tanks. Since I was the only one to work on getting out the rocks, I could only work on one hold at a time. That solved the problem on deck space for storing the oil drums.

While I was fishing out the rocks one by one, Huloo was experimenting on building a hand-operated suction pump with the bamboo poles savaged from our broken battens.

Just as I finished getting all the rocks out from under the first water tank and got back on deck to call it for the day, Cal and *Hsiao* Huang returned from their shore excursion.

"Who says there is no man on No Man Island?" Cal asked. "We found some human skeletons and a wreck."

"Never mind the skeletons. Go pump the bilge!" Huloo said to him.

"With what?"

Huloo handed him a two-foot long bamboo tube. It even had a handle. After trying it out, Cal exclaimed in disbelief.

"*Ta-ma-de,* it works!" We were all stunned to hear foul expression in Chinese coming out of the mouth of an American diplomat. He sure picked bad things up quickly. "It even pumps faster than that *ta-ma-de* motor pump. Where did you get it?"

"I made it."

"That *ta-ma-de* Huloo. What does he not know?"

"Okay, Hsiao Mai. We know you can swear in Chinese," Marco chuckled. "But do you know what *Huloo* means?"

"It's Huloo's name."

"No, it means gourd. The traditional Chinese medicine man uses *huloos* to store his medicines in. Since they come in different sizes, the medicine man never bothers to label them. But then you never know what medicine is inside the *huloo you got, ha, ha, ha, ha...*"

In the evening, I tried for the first time to send a message to FRA over the air in Morse code:

NR1 CK8 180755GMT

6697 7852 3966 9866 9398 8661 5611 3764

I had just learned that NR1 meant Message No. 1 and CK8 indicated the word count. Every navigator knew what 180755GMT stood for: on the 18th of the month at 7:55am Greenwich Mean Time. Each of the following 4-digit numbers was a code that I had looked up in the Standard Telegraph Codes Book to represent a Chinese character. It had taken me more time to look them up than sending the message. So I gave up and switched to English. I figured it would be much easier for the operator at the other end to look them up in an English-Chinese dictionary than for me to find the codes in that damned Telegraph book.

I spent the next two days in getting the rocks out of the bottoms of the other three water tanks. While I was crawling under the tanks, the rest of the crew had nothing to do. Cal went back on shore to scale the mountain. Benny went along with him. They returned to the junk with Benny thinking that this American was all right and Cal concluding that Benny knew about the junk and sailing better than any of us.

In the evening, I received this message from FRA:

> A TYPHOON HAS DEVELOPED IN THE CAROLINE
> ISLANDS EAST OF THE PHILIPPINES. TUNE IN TO
> WEATHER REPORT FOR MORE DETAILS

XVII

April 20, 1955

I got more information on the typhoon today. The pressure at its center was 990 mb. At noon it was positioned at 13°40'N, 135°20'E and moving toward NW at 9 knots.

The Junk's position at No Man Island was 25°45'N, 123°30'E. That put this tropical storm 1000 nautical miles from us. I told the boys that it was too far away to be concerned with. Anything could happen before it became a threat to us. It could wear off. It could land. It could veer off to the open sea. So we decided to wait for a while and see how it would develop before we make our move.

April 22, 1955

The typhoon had gotten a name now, Annie.

"Why do you Americans give names to typhoons?" Huloo asked our American crew. "We Chinese never do."

"How would you identify a typhoon then?" Cal asked him.

"Why female?"

"Because typhoons have the same temperament of women."

Our temperamental lady was centered at 16°30'N, 132°30'E today. She had not changed course, still moving NW at 9 knots, with gale force wind within a radius of 250 nautical miles. If she maintained the same course and speed, her front would reach our anchorage in 56 hours.

We must get out of here in time to get out of her way and to give the Yu Hsiang ample of time to return to Keelung.

"We should go back to Keelung as Mr. Chang has advised," said Benny.

80

"Are you out of your mind?" I could not keep my voice down. I was so surprised that Benny could knuckle down to officials so easily. That was not the Benny I knew. The Benny I knew was a rebel and a fighter like me.

"I'm just reasoning with rationale. You don't have to use your voice to overpower me. To be honest, we were never really prepared when we came out this time."

"How much more prepared do you want?"

"For example, the rocks and the water tanks."

I guessed the rocks and the water tanks were going to stick with me for the rest of my life.

"If you want to go back, you can go back by yourself," then Reno said. "The Yu Hsiang is still standing by there."

"Look, Benny..." we all tried to talk Benny out of whatever he was thinking. According to our mutual understanding at the beginning of this project, every decision must be made unanimously. So to return or not to return must be discussed among us even though only Benny was suggesting to return. The argument went on for quite a while. The two days of doing nothing at the anchorage made the crew antsy. The news on the approaching typhoon made everyone nervous. At the end, Benny was convinced (or coerced) to abandon his idea. Once the decision was made, there was no time to waste. We must set sail immediately. As to how to tell this to Mr. Chang, that was another matter. We left it to our spokesman, Marco.

"What if Mr. Chang insists we must return to Keelung?" Marco checked with us before going to Mr. Chang.

"Tell him we are being courteous to inform him. We don't have to. We will go on with or without his blessing."

"What if he refused to leave?"

"Then he'll have to sail with us."

"What should we do with the rest of the experts?"

"Put them on the Yu Hsiang."

"What if Mr. Chang asks the Yu Hsiang to force us to go back?"

"They won't listen to him."

"How do you know?"

"Fishermen always stick-up for one another."

Marco talked to Mr. Chang that night. However, it was Mr. Chang speaking most of the time. His monotone voice soon put me to sleep. They stayed in the galley talking all night.

Early next morning, we transported all our guests to the Yu Hsiang without any incidence. The Yu Hsiang towed us out of the anchorage. At about 4 miles east of No Man Island we parted tow. We raised sails and headed out to the Pacific. While we were raising the sails, the Yu Hsiang circled us. We could hear the junk expert, *Lao* Tseng, calling out to give us his last instruction, "Take in the mainsheets as much as you can. That way you may be able to sail closer to the wind. In this wind you may raise the mainsail all the way to the top. But don't forget to shorten it when the wind gets stronger."

The Yu Hsiang gave us a long farewell blast before heading back to Keelung. We felt so good. From now on we would be completely on our own. I felt like a chick-hawk finally leaving its mother and flying away from its nest. I entered the following in the logbook:

April 23, 1955 *9:00 am LCT (Taiwan)*
Ship's position: 4 nautical miles E of No Man Island
Ship's course E
Tacking between NE and SE, changing tack every hour
Atmospheric Pressure: 1014.5 mb
Temperature: 27.5°C
Wind: E at 1 B.S.
Visibility: Fine
Typhoon Annie center (990 mb): 18°20'N, 131°24'E,
With front 250 nautical miles from center moving NW at 9 knots

I felt seasick. We had been at anchorage too long. I put down everything that I was doing and climbed into my bunk.

It felt so good to be back in my own bunk. I had the best sleep in all the past eight months.

April 24, 1955

The typhoon center had moved to 19°42'N, 129°54'E, proceeding in the same NW direction with the same 9-knot speed. The junk's position at 1430 LCT was 25°35'N, 126°16'E, at a safe distance of 170 nautical miles from the front of this tropical low-pressure system.

When I got on the radio, I got a surprise message. It was an "order" from the General for us to return to Keelung. That did not sound like the General at all. Something was fishy. He had clearly told us not to return when he said he would help us to get the second sailing permit. Besides, after the failure of our first attempt, he did not order us to abort the trip. He only tried to talk us out. Considering it as advice, it was not a sound advice either. The distance to Keelung was twice as long as that to Okinawa. That had to be Mr. Chang's idea in the name of the General. I ignored it, pretending I had difficulty in receiving the message just like I had had on our first trip. I tapped on the Morse code key:

BEDM SIGNS OFF

XVIII

<u>April 25, 1955</u>

0800 LCT: Typhoon center at 20°50'N, 128°45'E
Junk's position 25°42'N, 126°35'E
Barometer reading 1017 mb
Wind NE 7 B.S.

The shifting of the wind from E to NE bothered me. That looked like the front of an advancing anti-clockwise cyclone. The increase in the strength of the wind (to over 60 miles an hour) reinforced my suspicion. What was still missing was the rain.

I realized that our junk's assumed position could be off by 50 to 100 miles when I was depending completely on dead reckoning to calculate my position. My last shot of the sun was taken 24 hours ago. Our last sight of land was two days ago. Until now, I still did not have enough data to estimate the leeway. It was quite tricky to make a guess when we had 2600 square feet of sails above water and only 3-foot draft and a 3'x 12' rudder under water. I figured that if we were making 10 knots in a 7 B.S. (44 knots) wind, the junk's speed was one quarter of the wind speed. Let us assume the leeway was one tenth of the wind speed, we would have been pushed sideway at 4 nautical miles per hour. In 48 hours we could be 200 miles off my dead reckoning position. Should I add that to the entry in the logbook? What if the leeway was only one hundredth of the wind speed? Then the leeway would only be 20 miles in 48 hours.

The wind was not terribly strong, not as strong as some of the gales I had seen on the China Coast. But the junk was flying on the huge waves. The long waves signaled the approach of a distant cyclone. (Waves generated by a cyclone traveled much faster than the cyclone itself.) They were big enough to toss an ocean liner like a toy. Being smaller than the wave, our junk took it easier than the big ships. She rode them, more or less, up and down. Our fore deck remained dry most of the time. Only when the waves broke up would the fore deck be submerged. But as time went on, more and more waves were breaking up.

The surface of the sea around us was now covered with a white netting of foam that was dragged out from the breaking waves by the wind. Our junk was like a butcher's knife cutting on beef tallow. The color of the water under the tallow was as black as that of a piece of rotten meat. Fast moving dark clouds covered up the entire sky, parting occasionally to let some streaks of sunlight shine on the boiling sea below.

Intermittent rain started to fall by midmorning. The force of the wind also increased, breaking up every wave. This was definitely Lady Annie. No mistake. But our own lady, the *Free China,* was not admitting defeat. The ship's log registered 10 knots. I tried to imagine that we were in a race. Only this time, we were racing against Lady Annie. Every time the junk was pushed by a roller from behind to lurch forward, the tip of the lowest batten on the mainsail would dip into the water. When she bounced back from a dipping, the crack at the base of the mainmast would widen. Although we had tied a shroud on the tack side, we could still put a hand into the crack when it opened up.

We started to worry, not about whether the junk could take it or not but about losing our mast. We must reef. That started a heated argument on deck.

Reno, Marco and Cal wanted to keep the sail up for a little while longer. (Cal entered the argument for the first time. He was too excited not to.) Benny, Huloo and I insisted that we must reduce the sail immediately.

While the junk was enjoying the run of her life, she was taking a beating on her windward side. Every time a sea hit, the mast would shake like a drumstick, sending a train of ripple through the sails. The impact could be felt through the tiller.

The tiller was the most sensitive part of the junk. It

counterbalanced a 3'x 12' rudder that not only held the heading of the vessel but also served as a centerboard. When the rudder was hit by a wave, no one was strong enough to hold down the tiller. So it must be lashed down. If it ever got loose, it would turn into the tail of a wild crocodile.

While we were arguing, the tiller-man suddenly cried out, "It broke!"

All the heads turned. We saw a limping tiller, still wrapped in the leash and under the armpit of the helmsman on one side, hanging at an angle to the rudderpost at the far end. The junk swung swiftly off her course. All the wind was spilled out of her sails. Like a well-trained horse, which always stopped when it lost its rider, the junk heaved to. As she rolled with the waves, the sail swept from one side to the other side across her beam. The unrestrained sheets dipped in and out of the water, tightening up as they reached their ends and sending sprays on us.

We were prepared this time. We had a spare tiller. We quickly replaced the broken tiller with the spare. In no time the junk sprung back on her course. Once again she started to ride the billowing seas like a horse on an obstacle race.

With the broken tiller, the opposition to shorten the sail finally gave in. We lowered the mainsail to one third. That eased the strain on the masts. The crack at the base of the mainmast was much smaller. But the speed was not much less. The ship's log still registered 8 knots. Of course, the wind had also increased somewhat in the mean time.

I went into the cabin to try to send a radio message to FRA. Before I get a contact, I heard that deadly cry on deck again, "Tiller broke!"

All hands rushed back on deck again. We quickly doused the sails. The junk pointed peculiarly with her stern into the wind. After giving it a little bit of thought, it immediately became obvious. There was a 3'x 12' rudder dragging in the water like a sea anchor.

The sea anchor!

Then someone remembered the extra triangular sail that we

could not figure out what it was for. It was probably the stern sail. But we had never been able to find the stern mast, although there was a hole on the poop deck probably for stepping it. We could have thrown it away during the repair. It did not matter. We got the sail out of the storage hold and tied one of its edges to a bamboo pole and the free corner to our anchor. There we had made ourselves a sea anchor.

We cast the sea anchor into the water and tied it on the bow. It pulled the boat sideway to broadside the weather at a right angle. That made the junk roll more and take in more water onto her deck.

Of course she broadsided. We had forgotten to hoist up the rudder, which was acting as a sea anchor at the stern. We hurriedly hoisted it up. It turned the stern more away from the weather all right. But being in the gudgeon, the rudder started to bang on the gudgeon whenever a sea hit rather than just turning in it freely as it supposed to do. If we let it go on like this, eventually either the rudder or the gudgeon would break. Here was the dilemma:

1. Do nothing and expose our stern to the weather;

2. Leave both the sea anchor and the rudder in the water and let the weather attack from our broadside;

3. Have just the sea anchor in the water and let the rudder bang on the gudgeon.

I let my fellow junk-mates argue this one out and went to my navigation corner to compose this message to FRA.

> NR14 250030 GMT
> PSN 25°42'N 126°35'E
> TILLER BROKEN NO STEERAGE

Marco came into the cabin and asked me to add a request:

> NR14 CK12 250030GMT
> PSN 25°42'N 126°35'E
> TILLER BROKEN NO STEERAGE
> URGENTLY REQUEST TOW TO OKINAWA

Before I started sending out the telegram, Cal came in and told us, "There is an American military base in Okinawa. Perhaps we can ask them for help."

"Why do you think they will help a Chinese junk?" Marco asked. "There are so many of them at sea."

"Because there is an American on board this one."

So the final message that went out read as follows:

DE BEDM
NR14 CK19 250030GMT PSN 2537N 12655E
TILLER BROKEN NO STEERAGE URGENTLY
REQUEST TOW TO OKINAWA ASK US NAVY
WIND NE7 1016.5MB

In the FRA response, Mr. Lai instructed me to add an "XXX" in front of my message and continue to repeat it every half an hour until rescue arrived.

I asked him what did "XXX" mean. He told me to stop asking "silly questions".

"Just do as I said."

What could I say? He was my mentor.

XIX

At about 3 pm I got a message from Mr. Lai. He informed us that a Chinese ship, the SS Chungking Victory, just happened to be in the vicinity. She had been steaming toward us since noon.

The Chungking Victory was a 10,000-ton Victory ship. She was the biggest ship ever owned by a Chinese steamship company.

Noon was three hours ago. These big ships had an over-20-knot speed. In three hours she would have covered at least 60 miles. That was a good half-day sailing for us at our average speed. Was that what they meant by *vicinity?* Having no steerage, we could only wait. While we were waiting, we had plenty of time to argue about our fate and what to do.

"How accurate is that position you have reported in your message?" Marco asked me.

"I don't know," I really did not know. "I could be off by 20 miles or by 200 miles. I have no way to check."

"What do you mean no way? Look, the sun is still peeping out from time to time. Can't you steal a quick shot at it?"

"Look at those waves around us. Each one is as tall as a three-story building. Can you see the horizon?"

"Can you just level your sextant the best you can and take a rough shot?"

"Are you kidding? Marco, don't talk like a land-lubber."

"Then how do you expect that Victory ship to find us among these towering waves? We are sitting as low as your wreck on Dongsha."

"What does the Victory have to do with a wreck on Dongsha?"

"Huloo had a precise position of that reef and, yet, he still could not find you."

"If he did not want to find me, what could I do?"

"It was not that I did not want to find you," Huloo said in defense. "I just did not want to get too close and end up on the reef like you did. Then there would have been two boats to be rescued."

"Sure," I said.

"The Chungking Victory could run into us just like you ran onto that reef," said Marco.

"She has a radar."

"What are you guys talking about?" Cal joined in our discussion. "Where is this wreck?"

"In South China Sea," Marco explained. "A few years ago Hsiao Chow put his boat on a reef there in a typhoon just like this. Huloo was sent out to rescue him. But he couldn't even find the reef."

"You mean it could happen to our rescue too?"

"Of course. Look at those billows. It's just like finding you in your California mountains." Cal had been telling us about hiking in the Sierra Mountains in California. He liked to compare sailing with mountain climbing.

"Didn't Huloo just say they have radar?"

"Radar operates on direct sights. How can they get a direct sight on us when we are hiding among these waves?"

"What shall we do then?"

"Just sit it out."

"Like this?"

"Like this."

"Right here?"

"Where else?"

"If this Chinese ship cannot find us, I am sure that one of our Navy ships will find us."

"Don't count on it," Marco said. Turning to me he said, "Hey, Hsiao Chow, you had better keep sending your message so that they can get a bearing on us with their direction finder."

"What is a direction finder?" Cal asked.

"It's a device that picks up a radio signal along the direction between the sender and the receiver."

"If they cannot find us by radar, why do you think they can find us by radio? Isn't radar a more advanced device?"

"A radio receiver does not need to sight the transmitter that sends out the signal. Radar does."

"Didn't Huloo have a direction finder?"

"No."

"Did Paul really put a boat on a reef?"

"Why do you think we were surprised to see you putting your life in our hands, ha, ha, ha, ha?"

We talked as if we were at a tea party. We laughed as if nothing was going to happen. But what was really going through each person's mind, we were not sharing.

At dusk, we sighted a speck on the horizon. In half an hour, she was at our side. A voice came through a loud speaker. It had a Cantonese accent like Benny's.

"This is the captain of the Chungking Victory. Are you ready to abandon ship?"

Abandon ship? What was he talking about? Mr. Lai had never mentioned it in his last radio message. It shocked us into a dead silence.

The muteness did not last very long though. An angry shouting burst out. Ignoring the outburst on our deck, the captain's calm voice came down again,

"Get ready to abandon ship."

The roaring seas must have covered our voices. I suddenly thought of the signal light that the FRA Slipway manager, Fung Chuang, had given me. I took it out and flashed these codes:

NO ABANDON SHIP

That must have shaken the captain. He came to his sanity and asked,

"What do you want?"

I flashed back.

NEED TOW TO OKINAWA

Then we heard this:

"Our obligation is to save lives, not your ship."

The Junk that Challenged the Yachts

We were all stunned. In all our 40 some combined years at sea, we had never heard of any response that was so insensitive and so lacking in feeling and compassion. Whenever we saw any disabled vessel at sea, in storm or in calm, we always gave her a tow to some safe place. I once even got a tow from a freighter as big as this one outside of Manila. We took survivors only if the vessel had abandoned the crew.

We could not believe that the old man on the Victory was so un-seamanlike. But if that was his conscience, what could we say? I flashed,

GO AWAY

She did not leave. She started to circle us and, at the same time, a younger voice came through the loud speaker urging us to abandon ship. I flashed a few more time,

STAY CLEAR

and then turned my signal light off.

The Chungking Victory stopped circling and took off in a NE course. We watched her in silence and in relief until she disappeared down the horizon.

The scene at the launching of the newly painted *Free China* reappeared before my eyes – the crowd, the speeches, the champagne, the foam on the slipway, the firecrackers, the cheers... I heard these words that I had read somewhere:

> *And lo, from the assembled crowd*
> *There rose a shout, prolonged and loud,*
> *That to the ocean seemed to say:*
> *Take her, O bridegroom, old and grey;*
> *Take her to thy protecting arms,*
> *With all her youth and all her charms.*

We were now indeed in his arms. The seas were climbing all over us.

I went to turn on the radio. It was still set on 8.5MC. I could hear the weather report coming out of the scratchy speaker. I switched it to 8714 kc. I heard *Hsiao* Huang, the radio expert who had come out with the evaluation team to advise us on radio, calling us. I acknowledged. Then he said, "Inspector Lo wants to speak to you."

Inspector Lo Cheng-San was the official Security Officer representing the Garrison Command to monitor all the radio communication among the fishing boats in Taiwan. Regardless of his high position, he preferred to hang around the fishermen than to mingle in the office, probably because he was a big drinker. Most fishermen were big drinkers. We knew him very well.

"Hsiao Chow," Inspector Lo's voice came through the speaker. "Ask all the boys to come to the radio. Listen to me carefully. Chairman Chen Liang and the highest authority in Taipei order you to abandon the *Free China* and go immediately on board the Chungking Victory. The typhoon is heading your way. There is no time to lose. The highest authority says that you boys have gone too far. You must stop right now. There is nothing disgraceful in abandoning ship. Did you hear me?"

Too late. I tapped out the response in codes:

THANKS YOU BEDM SIGNS OFF

Inspector Lo's voice immediately bounced back on air,

"Listen to me, Hsiao Chow..."

I looked at the junk's registration plate nailed on the bulkhead. Under Owner of the Vessel, I saw my name. Then I thought: I had not violated any law on land. I had not violated any international law on high sea. I was on my own boat. I was free. I did not have to listen to anybody. I switched off the radio.

What shall we do next? A conference was assembled on the poop deck. We realized that we had done everything there was to be done to ride out the typhoon. But we should think about what to do after the typhoon. We needed a tiller to steer. Huloo immediately went to work on refitting the broken tiller. We had no saw on board. So he had to make do with a chisel.

"That would take forever," said Marco as he watched Huloo chiseling away. Then he went inside the cabin and got the fire ax. "Let me do it."

In no time, Marco shaved the end of the broken tiller into a perfect fit to the rectangular hole on the rudder.

"Where did you learn that?" we asked in surprised. Marco was the last person on board one would expect to do anything with his hand.

"In my grandfather's house in Northern China, we burned lots of firewood in wintertime," he said. "The large tree trunks had to be chopped into smaller pieces. That was my job."

We placed our watch one at the bow to watch the sea anchor and one at the stern. We had no navigation lights and no sail to shine on to let an approaching ship see us. We only had a signal light. That was enough. We would watch out for them. Not too many ships were going to be at sea in a typhoon anyway.

Benny and I took the 10pm to 2am watch. At 11:00pm, we sighted a light. We kept a close watch on it. At 11:15, we could see her running lights. She was heading toward us at a good speed. At 11:20, I called all hands on deck. At 11:30, I started flashing them,

DISABLED KEEP AWAY

She did not seem to heed our warning. At 11:40pm, the approaching ship suddenly heaved to. Her masts lit up like a Christmas tree. Her deck lit up as bright as a basketball game at night, illuminating the white-capped seas around her like snow-capped peaks in a mountain range. We could see black dots lining up the railing on her main deck like ants around the brim of a candy jar. It was too dark to see her name. Then a light started blinking from her bridge. I read it aloud to my fellow shipmates:

ARE YOU READY TO ABANDON SHIP

I'll be damned! It was that *bi-yang-de* Chungking Victory again. Was that what she had come back for? To ask us the same question again? Wasn't our last message clear enough? If we had refused to abandon ship then, why would he think we were going to abandon ship six hours later?

NO

I flashed back. I skipped "STAY AWAY" this time. Then the following flashes were exchanged between us:

TYPHOON ANNIE IS 60 MILES AWAY
ROGER THANKS
GET READY TO ABANDON SHIP

94

    NO
Silence
    ARE YOU READY
    NO ABANDON SHIP
Silence again. When her light started blinking again, I read aloud the following codes so that my shipmates could hear:
    GET READY TO RECEIVE TOW

XX

The tow was worse than the pounding by the typhoon. We thought our foremast was going to be pulled out of its base. Our bow kept dipping into our own bow wave. The Victory kept a spotlight on us throughout the tow. The submerged towline jumped out of the water several times. After each time, the Victory would pay out more rope. Could she run out of rope?

Luckily Marco had refitted the broken tiller into the rudderpost so that we could steer. Otherwise we would have been running like a sailfish caught on a troll line, dashing wildly from side to side.

Actually the tow did not start until 2am. The Victory had had a hard time in passing the towline to us. She was 10,000 tons and we were only 20 tons. She could not get too close to us or she would crush us into pieces.

She first tried to shoot a heave line to us. When that failed, she tried to circle us with the heave line tied to an oil drum. The drum kept being blown away. Being the recipient, we were not in the position to offer any advice. Finally someone on the Victory wised up and realized that the oil drum had the highest freeboard, so-to-speak, considering it was floating completely on the surface of the water. The freighter had the next highest freeboard and the junk, being low, had the least. So they filled the oil drum with 90% water and tied a life buoy with a light onto it. Being mostly submerged this time, the drum was not subjected to the blowing of the wind and stayed put in the water. After dropping the drum and heave line, supported by a few empty oil drums this time, to our windward side, the Victory steamed to our downwind. The heave line was dragged slowly to cross our bow. We picked it up and pulled until we got the towline.

The tow lasted all night and the next morning. At noon we entered Naha, the capital of Okinawa. The Chungking Victory dropped her anchor and we pulled up to tie alongside her. She was huge. Our mast did not even reach her deck. A rope ladder was dropped down to us. Marco, Benny and Cal climbed up.

Half an hour later, Marco and Cal returned to the junk.

"Guess what?" Cal said excitedly. "All the passengers on the Victory knew me. They had all been to my office for visas. They are students going to study in America. But I could only recognize a few."

"Yeah, only the girls, ha, ha, ha, ha," said Marco. "What did you call that cute one? Hsiao Peiping? Never mind that. The captain was mad at us. He repeated to me that he did not have the obligation to give us a tow. He said this would cost his company a lot of money."

Money, that was all these merchantmen could think of. He scolded Marco for refusing to obey the order of the high authority in Taipei.

"I took the blame for you, Hsiao Chow," Marco said to me. "He chewed me up for reporting an erroneous ship's position. I did not tell him that you were the navigator. He said we were 50 miles off."

"Only 50 miles?" I could not believe it. "That means my dead reckoning was not too bad."

"He told me he had received two telegrams from the Minister of Transportation, one instructing him to hand the junk to the port authority of Naha and one to the port authority of Naha to detain our junk and repatriate the crew. What shall we do?"

No one had an answer.

Benny returned to the junk an hour later. It turned out that the captain of the Victory was the brother of the principal of the marine college that Benny had attended. He asked Benny to stay after Marco and Cal had left.

"Captain Yao said that the North Pacific is so rough that we would not have a chance to survive."

"That's nothing new," I said. "Cap and those retired sea captains who interrogated me have said the same thing."

"He asked me to persuade you not to go on. Then he urged me personally not to go on if you guys were crazy enough to ignore his advice."

"Well, what did you say to him?" Reno asked.

"I did not say anything. He certainly knows the sea better than any of us."

"Bull shit!" Huloo poked his head into the cabin to express his contempt.

"I just listened. But I think he's got a point."

"Tell it to yourself. Don't tell us."

"Trouble with you, Reno, is that you don't listen and you don't use your head."

"You call being scared using your head?"

"Did I say I was scared?"

"What you just said sure sounded to me like that."

"Cut it out," Marco stepped in to stop the dogfight. "Get ready to receive a tow from that tug."

After we were tied down to the dock, a uniformed American came on board and asked, "Who is the navigator?"

"I am," I proudly presented myself.

"We dispatched sea tugs and sea planes to look for you at the ship's position you gave in your radio message. They searched the area thoroughly and couldn't see a damn thing."

I was so embarrassed that I wished I could find a hole to hide. Thank God, Marco came to my rescue.

"Thank you very much. It's all right. A merchantman found us, ha, ha, ha, ha!"

For the first time, Marco's casual laugh sounded so heart warming and comforting to me.

XXI

No one in this place understood what we were speaking. We had to communicate either in English or, mostly, by waving our hands. We suddenly realized that we were not in China any more. We were now in Okinawa.

Okinawa had always sounded exotic to me. It was seceded to Japan by China in 1874 and now occupied by the United States since the Japanese surrender in 1945. I was surprised to see the native people looking just like us. I had had the impression that they were Polynesians with dark complexion and brown hair like those seaweed divers I met on Dongsha, where I shipwrecked a few years back. Now thinking in retrospect, their complexion must have been caused by long exposures to the tropical sun and the salt water. I probably looked the same to my rescuers when they found me.

While in Naha, we had two urgent matters to attend to.

Since Okinawa was occupied by the Americans, we figured that Cal would be the ideal person to deal with the local authority. He had all the qualifications: a compatriot (fellow American), an intellectual (college graduate), a comrade (ex-marine) and a diplomat (vice consul). Plus he had studied International Relations in some advanced school.

"Cal, here is an assignment for you," Marco said to him. "Go get a clearance for us to leave this port as soon as we are ready."

"How would I do that?" Cal asked at a total loss.

"Isn't there an American expression, by hook and by crook, ha, ha, ha, ha?"

With the clearance taken care of, we turned our attention to the other matter.

"What shall we do about the tiller?" Marco brought it up to the crew.

"Find a carpenter to make one."

"Just one?"

"Several."

"How many?"

"Six."

"Is six enough?"

"How about...?"

"Nothing is enough," Huloo interceded. "On the other hand, one is enough, if we know how to handle it. How do you think the former crew has sailed the junk for so many years with just one tiller? Fifty years, wasn't that what the one-eye Ou Ah-lin estimated? We just have to figure out a way to cushion it when a sea hits."

We finally agreed in making six new tillers and two shock absorbers, one on each side.

The design Huloo had proposed was quite simple and straightforward. There was nothing to argue about. It consisted of a steel tube fitted with a spring and a steel rod inside. But an argument emerged just the same. How big, how thick and how long should the spring be? When it was shortened, which we might have to do to adjust it to the real situation at sea, would its strength increase or decrease?

"Let's look at a yoke," Huloo suggested. "When it is shortened, it bounces faster on the shoulder."

"Eh, a farmer is always a farmer," Reno said. "We are on a boat, Huloo, not a farm."

The argument went on and on. But Benny did not say a word. He had become so quiet and secluded since his last quarrel with Reno. He even lost his appetite and sleep. Finally he asked me to help him write a telegram to Gen. Chen Liang. (Telegrams outside of China must be written in English and Benny's English was limited to *Thank you* and *Good Morning.*) He got a reply on the following day. Suddenly Benny became himself again and started to talk and laugh and to engage in all our arguments.

"What did the general say?" We were all curious.

"He said no one should act on his own. We should act as a group."

So after all, the General was consistent in his support of our venture. Should we ignore the Minister's letter then? But almost simultaneously, Marco received a telegram from the General urging us to abort the trip. He said he was sending Inspector Lo to talk to us.

Inspector Lo arrived on the next day. Once again, I had to give up my bunk. We were not at sea. So no one stood watch. I could only spread out my Navy coat on the rice sacks like Marco did for Mr. Chang.

Inspector Lo was from Hunan. Food in that area was heavily spiced with hot peppers. Luckily we were not at sea. We went to local market and bought lots of red peppers. Benny, the best cook among us, volunteered to cook during the whole time Inspector Lo was on board. We asked Cal to get some good Scotch whisky and French cognac from the American military commissary. We asked Marco to be Inspector Lo's drinking mate. "We are in port," Huloo said to him. "Now you can drink to your heart's content." That made Marco's day and left all the crew's curses on the captain behind.

Finally on May 2, 40 days to the starting of the race, we were towed out of Naha harbor by a Caltex tug. It turned out that we only had the six tillers made. We could not find a blacksmith in Naha to make the shock absorbers. But we did find a hand-cranked cast iron suction pump for our bilge. Since it looked most likely we would not be able to make it to the race in 40 days, we decided to make a quick stop in Japan to have the shock absorbers made and to refill our water tank before going on to cross the Pacific. It just happened that Mr. Tsai, the manager of FRA, was in Tokyo to oversee the building of the long-distance long-line fishing boats the General had mentioned. He could help us to find a blacksmith. But we did not have any charts for those waters. I mentioned it to the captain of a Caltex tanker, which was tied near us. He kindly gave me a set of pilot charts for Tokyo Bay.

How did Cal convince the harbor authority to let us go? How did Marco talk Inspector Lo into giving us his blessing and sending a favorable telegram to Gen. Chen Liang? I had no idea and I did not want to know. All I cared about was that we were now at sea.

XXII

Benny and I were seasick on the first day out. We had stayed at anchorage too long. Every time I went to sea after a long stay in port, if the sea was rough I would always get seasick on the first day. I felt great on the second day and decided to send a message to FRA (XSX) via any ship at sea (CQ):

> CQ DE BEDM QSP TO XSX NR16 CK27 JUNK FREE CHINA 030750GMT PSN 2735N 12913E WIND S4 FINE ETA YOKOHAMA MAY10 ALL PSE WRITE MR TSAI OUR ETA PSE THANK CHEN LIANG FOR WHAT HE HAS DONE FOR US

We had three days of good sailing. We could feel the Kuroshio Warm Current through its tempting water temperature and the 372 glorious miles we had logged in during that time. We couldn't have made that much without the push by the Kuroshio. Then on the fourth day we were becalmed 80 (nautical) miles off the Kyushu shore.

"Listen, I'm going to take a dip," said Cal. "Who's going to join me?"

No one but Marco responded.

"You coming, Reno?"

"I don't know how to swim."

"How many years have you been fishing?" Cal could not believe what he had just heard. "What would you do if we had a shipwreck?"

"If we had a shipwreck on the ocean, everyone would die, swim or not swim. You think you can swim to America?"

"He won't even be able to swim back to the boat if the wind

kicks up," Huloo commented. "Look, guys, our sails are still up and our sheets are still tied down. We won't wait for you."

Sure enough, the air started to move only fifteen minutes after Marco and Cal plunged into the Kuroshio. Marco was close enough to reach the side of the boat. We threw him a rope. But nowhere could we see Cal. As soon as Marco got back on deck, the sails filled up to their full capacity. The junk swung around and took off on her own.

"Douse the sail!" more than one voice rose up.

Benny loosened the main halyard. The sail remained adhering to the mast. Huloo loosened the main sheet and then climbed up the thwarts on the fantail to look for Cal.

There he was, holding on a rope that was trailing behind the stern like a dead tuna on a hook line.

"Won't you listen to me from now on?" Huloo scolded Cal after pulling him back up on deck. "If we had not had that line trailing in the water, you would have joined the porpoises."

"My dear Sail Master Huloo," Cal said at perfect ease with a big smile on his face. "I was not as stupid as you think. I saw that line lying on deck. So I threw it in before getting into the water. Oh, of course, after you had warned us that the wind could kick up any time."

Cal was a true diplomat.

He landed in Naha without knowing anybody. Yet during the six days we were there, every day he would bring some new friends on board to meet us. Among them there was a Capt. Kilkenny who had had a ketch built in Naha that he planned to sail around the world. He suggested we take the junk back to Hong Kong to have her decorated with Oriental carvings before sailing to America. "She is not presentable to the Americans in her present look," he told us. There was this tall guy Pomeroy with a pretty wife, who always carried a boat on top of his car. He insisted in helping us to pump up our rubber raft to check for leaks. There was an Italian who wanted to travel through the ancient silk-road on camel back one day. He said he had flown over the road on an open-cockpit two-seater a few years ago to check its condition.

"There are plenty of pagodas along the road to serve as lighthouses to travelers," he told us. Then there was a bunch of cub scouts.

The breeze did not last very long. The sea became calm again an hour later. For the next three days, we went through several cycles outside of Kyushu and Shikoku from calm to fair sailing to near gale force blowing and then back to a dead calm. The junk was constantly transforming between a staggering drunken sailor and a racing porpoise.

Huloo thought we should make a Japanese flag for our stop-over in Japan. Luckily the Japanese flag was just a red dot on white. We found a piece of red cloth that came with some departure gift. I supplied the white cloth, which I had brought with me for making underpants. Huloo sewed them together.

With this kind of sailing, I had to stop reporting our Estimated Time of Arrival in Yokohama.

May 12, 1955

At three o'clock in the morning, I was wakened by the call of "All hands on deck!" Two tillers had snapped in a matter of minutes. The helmsman was steering with the third tiller through towering seas that were climbing onto the fore deck and turning it into a pond. The rain was hitting the sails almost horizontally making them look like two big white waterfalls. It was worse than Typhoon Annie. We were being overtaken by every angry sea that came rolling in from behind. They lifted us up some 30 feet high and then dumped us down and buried us with their wrath of white horses. One good thing about being on a sailing boat rather than a diesel boat was we did not hear the free-wheeling of the propeller when our stern was being lifted up.

"You have to ease up the tiller fast when a sea hits," Huloo told the one manning the tiller.

"I did. But when you felt it in your hand it was too late."

"I told him that he had wrapped the tiller too many times," the helmsman's mate registered his blame.

"It was loosely wound. It can slide."

105

"But..."

No time to argue or to blame. We tried to douse the mainsail. It wouldn't come down. Huloo climbed up the mast and lashed a downhaul on the gaff. We finally brought the mainsail down to just three battens.

"Why so much and so soon?" Reno complained. Reno was a gambler. Gambling was in his blood. In sailing, canvas was his stake, speed was his take and the mast was what he gambled on.

"We don't want to lose our mast at this time."

"Let's heave to," suggested Marco.

"No, we must keep moving. It's dangerous not to have any steerage in this area," I warned. "We are too close to shore."

"What shore?"

"Iro Saki."

Iro Saki is a cape off the SE coast of Kyushu to the SW of the entrance of Tokyo Bay where we were heading.

"Isn't there a lighthouse on it?"

"Yes."

"Why can't we see it?"

"In this visibility?"

"Then let's head out a little bit."

"We can't. I am trying to bring her through the passage between Iro Saki and Mikomoto Shima."

"While we cannot see either of them?"

"That's why we must have good steerage to react when we see something."

"Are you sure of where we are?" Marco must be thinking of the ship's position I erroneously reported when we were disabled in Typhoon Annie but did not want to spell it out.

"I had a pretty good fix last evening."

"How wide is this passage?"

"One mile."

No one argued with me when they heard this. Everyone started to look out for this Iro Saki. Then it happened again. I did not hear it. I just noticed the limping stick under the helmsman's arm. Luckily dawn was already breaking out.

"Douse the sail!"

"No! We must keep her moving."

"We are going to run onto the rocks."

"Do you see it? Where is it?"

"We are way off course!"

As everyone was voicing his opinion, Huloo grabbed the sheets and pulled them in as fast as he could. Even with a non-functioning rudder, the junk responded by pointing her bow into the wind. Then he gradually released the ropes in his hand. The junk slowly fell off the wind until she was pointing roughly along the course. In the meantime, someone got our last tiller out and stuck it into the rudderpost.

"Where the hell did you learn that, Huloo?" I asked in surprise when things settled down.

"I didn't learn that. I just tried."

"Where did you get the idea?"

"I flew kites a lot when I was a kid. We always tried to cut each other's line by playing our lines."

Then someone yelled out,

"Rock!"

It was four points off our port bow at about half a mile away. It was big. We could never run onto it even if we were closer. I was relieved to vaguely see a white structure on top of the huge cliff. But it was already daylight, too bright to see any flashes.

"If that is Iro Saki Lighthouse," I said. "Mikomoto Shima should be on our right. Then we would be heading straight for Tokyo Bay."

Before long, some shadow of rock showed up on our right in the misty rain. We raised the mainsail all the way to the top. We not only gained speed but a better control on the steerage. But that put a lot of torque on the mainmast and the tiller. Realizing it was our last tiller, Marco immediately got the ax out to fit a broken tiller as a spare. I went into the cabin and sent out this short message to FRA:

CQ DE BEDM QSP TO XSX NR26 CK22 120750GMT

The Junk that Challenged the Yachts

PSN SAGAMI NADA WIND SSW 7BS HOVE TO IN
HEAVY RAIN STORM AND HEAVY SEA ETA
YOKOHOMA
13 MORNING FOR REPAIRS

"Rocks!" the call brought me on deck.

"What are those?" the watch pointed at some black objects in the distance and asked.

"Strange! The pilot chart does not show any rocks," I said in great astonishment.

We decided to post lookouts on the bow. Huloo, Calvin and I went forward. It was already broad daylight. More rocks came up. We could see them very clearly. That reminded me of sailing inside the lagoon on Dongsha. The difference was these rocks were huge and sticking above the water while the coral pinnacles in Dongsha were small and under water.

"Why didn't you get a better chart that shows all these rocks?" Calvin asked me while we were perched on the bow to look out for more rocks.

"Our sailing chart for the Pacific does not even show Iro Saki or Mikomoto Shima. If we had not gotten these pilot charts from that Caltex captain, we would have to feel through these waters just like Zheng He, Columbus and Magellan."

"No wonder Benny told me that we were not prepared."

"No junk sailor has ever seen a chart in his entire life."

Marco went on watch at four in the afternoon. He was having such fun in steering in the strong wind that when Reno went to replace him at eight, like a child clinging to a new toy, he refused to yield the tiller to Reno.

"*Lao* Tseng said only the *laoda* is allowed on the tiller in these tricky waters," Marco quoted the junk expert who sailed with us from Keelung to No Man Island. "I am the *laoda* on this boat.*"

Reno did not want to fight with Marco. "Eh, let him have his kicks!"

As we got into Tokyo Bay, the sea calmed down. But we

started to encounter heavy traffic in narrower waters while the wind was just as strong as before. Instead of watching for the big rollers from behind, we were now watching out for big ships ahead. We did not know the rules of the roads for Tokyo Bay. We simply went by those for the Whampoo River that led into Shanghai, namely the big ships had the right of way. We had to make lots of tacking to avoid collisions.

Huloo, Calvin and I kept our lookout post on the bow with a hand-held running light. Huloo kept Marco informed as to where to turn and when to tack. Calvin would light up the foresail with a flashlight for on-coming vessels to see. I stood by to send signals to warn them that we were *DISABLED* and they should keep away from us. Benny posted himself by the sheets on the foresail and Reno on the mainsheets for instantaneous tacking.

Sailing through Tokyo Bay seemed to me to be as long as the tow covered by the Chungking Victory, in distance and in time. Shortly after midnight, we quietly slipped inside the breakwater of Yokohama harbor and dropped our anchor. Huloo hung up his hand-sewn Japanese flag on the foremast before turning in.

XXIII

<u>May 13, 1955</u>

Barely at the crack of dawn, a motor launch pulled alongside the junk. A black uniformed officer came on board and bent his waist in a 90-degree bow to us. Seeing our deck still littered with broken bamboo poles and uncoiled ropes, he shook his head and asked politely in English with a heavy Japanese accent,

"How dida you comu through dat stormu?"

"Barely."

He told us that was the worst storm they had ever had in recent years. A ferryboat had capsized and many passengers had been drowned. Then he took a glance at his wristwatch and quickly scratched something on a piece of paper. As he handed it to us, he noticed the Japanese flag on the foremast. He stared at it with a curious look. He had probably noticed the stitches. He stuck up his thumb and smiled at us. Then he gave us another right-angle bow before returning to his motor launch. The paper bore the letterhead of "Quarantine Service" and what he had scratched was: "*Pratique granted 0515 May 13, '55*"

Such politeness, such formality, such efficiency, such early working hour, and so considerate! Everything was so proper and precise as the ticking second hand on his wristwatch. Is this Japan?

Shortly after the quarantine boat left, the Immigration boat came, then the Customs boat. The Customs officer told us that we were not supposed to anchor there and asked us to move. We told him we needed a tow. An expression of surprise showed on his face. We explained to him that we did not know how to maneuver in narrow waters. The surprise expression on his face turned into a look of disbelief.

"You came through that storm and you don't know how to maneuver this boat?"

"Strong wind," Marco said. Then he wet his finger with his mouth and stuck up in the air and said, "Too weak, ha, ha, ha, ha."

We got a tow. We were towed pass a row of big ships to a dock where a huge crowd was gathered. It turned out that all the school children in Yokohama China Town had come out to greet us. Then some black uniformed Japanese students showed up. Later we were driven to the Chinese Ambassador's, Tung Hsien-Kwang, residence for lunch. What had we done that merited such an honor? Our ignorance in sailing as accused by Capt. Yao or our negligence in preparation as pointed out by Mr. Chang? I just hoped that the reporters here wouldn't bombard us with embarrassing questions.

June 15, 1955

The storm we'd just been through caused more damage than the typhoon. It did not de-mast us but it had surely pounded everything loose. The tiller and all its spares were broken, the sails were torn and chafed, the masts wobbled, the rudder loosened, many battens cracked and the junk sprung a leak. We must have her hauled up to see if the pounding had not cracked open some planking or knocked loose the rudder gudgeon. We found a boatyard right here in Yokohama. But it did not want to touch the junk fearing that if something went wrong at sea later, it could be held responsible. We finally found one, Azuma Boat Co., in the neighboring Yokosuka, a naval port for the American Navy.

The junk was hauled up on the slipway. Thank Heaven, both the planking and the gudgeon were intact. But a lot of old dry caulking had been knocked out and the gudgeon was loose. After we had all those things taken care of, we added some features. We had two shock absorbers made; we ordered more spares for the tiller; across the top of our cabin, we installed an iron guard with a dip in the middle big enough to cradle the bundle of furled mainsail and the battens so that we did not have to throw our bodies onto it every time we lower the sail. Then we added two naturally grown tree-knees, one on each side of the mainmast, to reinforce its base. Hopefully that would prevent the gap in the base to widen further when under stress.

During this time, an officer from a marine radio station of the Japanese Maritime Safety Guard Bureau, JGC, paid us a visit. He told us that because we were too far from Keelung to keep in contact with our home station, they were volunteering to be our contact from now on. When we got out of their range, a San Francisco station, KFS, would take over. To me personally, that meant from now on, I would have to receive messages in Morse code. So far all the radio messages I had received from Keelung (XSX) were in voice. Although I had been sending my messages in Morse code, I had the control of the speed. In receiving, I would be at the mercy of the other operator.

When we received the repair bill, we were flabbergasted. We had not realized that the cost of slipway and labor could be that much higher than those in Taiwan. It was barely ten years since their surrender. Their labors were now being paid so well while our labor force in Taiwan was still struggling.

No pay, no letting our boat into water.

Luckily the General Manager of FRA, Tsai Tsung Hsieng, was still in Tokyo. Out of desperation, we went to see him.

"Let me go with you to Yokosuka," Mr. Tsai said.

It took Mr. Tsai just a few minutes talking to Mr. Watanabi, the owner of Azuma Boat Co. We were immediately let down into the water. I could not understand a word of what he had said. It was all in Japanese.

"How are we going to pay you back?" we asked Mr. Tsai.

"Let's not talk about that now," he said. "Just concentrate in getting your junk to sea."

We suddenly realized why those school children came out to the dock on our arrival. They did not come to greet us. They came to see the junk *Free China*. She represented the spirit of all those people who had helped to put the junk to sea.

The first face that came to my mind was the General, **Chen Liang**, followed by those of my two mentors, **Mr. Lai Jun-Cheng** in radio operation and **Capt. L. Bosshardt** in navigation.

Then these names appeared one after another: **Mr. G. W. Blunt White**, who invited us to the race; **Capts. Chang Chang-Hai, Dai Hsian-Ying** and **Yao Huan-Rui,** who offered us risky tows on high sea; **Dr. Liu Rui-Heng**, who sought me out and introduced me to the mayor of Keelung; **Mayor Hsieh Kuan-Yi**, who helped us find a junk; **Governor Yan Chia-Kan**, who donated 45,000 yuan toward the purchase of the junk; **Attorney Lin Fang**, who drafted the contract for title transfer of the junk; **Mr. Shen Ti-Hsian** supervised the repairs and did the artwork on the bow, the fantail and the cabin; **Mr. Sha Song-Tao** and his staff at the FRA Net Loft helped us make the new sails; **Legislator Wang Shin-Heng** obtained the crew's passports; **Harbor Master Hsu Ren-Shou** facilitated the ship's papers; **Mr. Pao G. Shen** deposited $2500 in an American bank as collaterals for our US visas; **Capt. Yeh Shih-Hsiang**, who adjusted our compass and convinced the investigation committee on our seaworthiness and, regardless what my general feeling toward journalists was, the reporter from Central News, **Song Yue**, whose reports had opened many doors to us.

I looked around the boat, every item reminded me of its donor. The winter clothes on our bodies were provided by **Admiral Liang Hsu-Chao**; the life saving equipment including a lifeboat compass that we were depending on to guide us across the oceans came from **Capt. Chase**; the 5HP diesel engine was a gift from **Monsieur Lin Jun-Li**; the ship's compass that was knocked overboard was from **Capt. Yang Tsi-Hsun**, thanks just the same; the pennants and the signal light that enabled us to communicate with our rescue on the high sea were from **Capt. Fung Chuang**; my sextant was a gift from **Capt. Lin Shu-Lung**; the chronometer was from **Capt. Wang Uh**; 1000 vitamin C pills donated by **Mr. Wu Jing-Shuan**; 2 kg pork lard to slush the mast was given by **Mr. Lin Fung-Chu**; the portable short-wave radio that served as our only ears to the outside world was loaned to me by **Mrs. James Hunter**; the spare radio transmitter was provided by **Mr. Lo Cheng-San**, who also visited us in Naha, Okinawa; the patent log that logged over 20,000 nautical miles for our 7,000-mile voyage was from **Capt. Ma Lian-Ching**.

Then there were these faceless donors, behind each of them there were many faces: **Fisheries Rehabilitation Administration**, which provided slipway and repair services; **Rotary Clubs** of Keelung, Taipei E and Taipei W donated ship's provisions for 5 months; **MAAG (Major General William C. Chase) gave us** many cases of American treats; **Joint Commission on Rural Reconstruction (ECA)** gave us 15 gallons of dehydrated vegetables; **Hsian Da Wang (Mr. Yao Jun-Chi)** gave us spices, soy sauce and chili sauce; **Chung Hwa Paint Store**, donated 20 gallons of paint; **Yung Ku Paint Store** gave us 30 gallons of paint; **Gong Cheng Hardware Store, Heng Mao Hardware Store** and **Yi Lung Hardware Store** supplied us all the necessary machinery and carpentry tools except a saw; **Keelung Harbor Office** gave us 50 empty 50-gallon drums; **Caltex** supplied us the charts for Yokohama & vicinity; **Western Enterprise (Capt. Barkus)** gave us an inflatable rubber raft to replace our leaky 50-year-old sampan; **U.S. Navy Sea Rescue** dispatched seaplanes and sea tugs in the typhoon to search for us; **SS Chungking Victory**, which finally found us and towed us out of the typhoon; **Commissary at Military Assistance Advisory Group** donated 2500 feet of 16 mm Kodachrome film to record our voyage; **FRA Radio Station XSX** installed a radio transmitter TCS-13 that enabled us to maintain radio contact with shore throughout the voyage; **Marine Radio Coastal Station JGC** (Yokohama) and **Marine Radio Coastal Station KFS** (Pt. Reys, California) volunteered to be our contacts while we were unreachable by XSX (Keelung) in the Pacific. Now **Mr. Tsai** got our boat into the water.

Not until this moment did I realize that these people helped us without any motivation. It was neither political nor commercial. Like us, they simply wanted to see a Chinese junk sail on big oceans. The name *Free China* did not represent this spirit. It carried a political tone. If this was a free China, there must be a non-free China somewhere. Perhaps the *Spirit of Taiwan* would have been a more appropriate name.

Paul Chow

<u>June 17, 1955</u>

Our quick stop in Japan turned into a 36-day tie-up in Yokosuka. I was so glad that we were finally ready to leave, although I would certainly miss my evening hot bath in the unisex bathhouse that its owner invited us to visit every day free of charge and the freedom to go on shore at any time when I tried to get out of my shipmates' faces. I would also miss the sound of Japan, where women spoke like canaries, men bellowed like sea lions and music out of the loud speakers on the streets sounded like breeze blowing through a bamboo forest.

There was a small party gathered at the boatyard to see us off. Besides some officials from the Chinese Embassy, there were our new friends with whom we could only communicate with hands: Marco's drinking friend, Lao Tu, the bathhouse owner, the noodle shop owner, the barber, the fishmonger at the fresh food market, the fishermen and artists on the waterfront and the workers at the boatyard. I would miss their muted friendly smiles.

On the other side of the boatyard dock was another small group of farewell wishers. Contrary to our traditional-clad friends, these people were better dressed, men in suits and women in western dresses and prettily made up. They were Calvin's friends from the big city Tokyo.

"How many girls in tears did you leave in this port, sailor?" Marco asked Cal when he saw some of these women wiping their eyes and covering up their mouths.

"Chue ni ma de!" Cal cursed in Chinese while laughing it off.

It was a shame on us that up to this time we still did not know how to handle the sails in narrow waters. To our great embarrassment in front of all these well-wishers, we were being towed away from the dock by a U.S. Navy landing craft.

While under tow, my minds was preoccupied with the race that we had missed. It had started five days ago. Was it a blessing or a regret? If we had not run into that typhoon and the storm outside of Japan, we would have made it. But could we really make it if we had set sail in April, the month that Cap had warned

115

to be nasty and murderous?

Nevertheless we could still challenge a race across the Pacific. The Pacific was a much larger body of water than the Atlantic. But according to that guy Folster, whom Cal had met in Tokyo and brought out to see the junk, the Pacific in June and July was nothing but cold, rain, fog and calm. How many days did it take him to sail across the Pacific in his ketch? Forty-eight days? There were 4,565 nautical miles (5,257 statute miles) from Yokosuka to San Francisco. If we could average 100 nautical miles a day, we would be able to break that record. That shouldn't be too hard to do.

While we were mingling with noodle shop owners and fishmongers on the waterfront, Cal was hobnobbing in the higher society of diplomats and intellectuals in Tokyo. He had brought many of them on board besides Folster. They nodded or bowed or shook hands with us politely. But none of them introduced themselves or asked our names except this American lady, Ann Rhorer. She gave us a Jolly Roger. "In case you ran out of provisions at sea, you might need this to stop some ship to borrow some grocery," she said. What a considerate thought!

Once we were cast off in Tokyo Bay, we felt like a hooked fish being released and thrown back into the sea. Having tacked through its traffic at night when we came in, sailing in the Tokyo Bay during broad daylight was a breeze. But the weather was not helpful. Even with the ebb tide, it took us a big portion of the day to get out of the Tokyo Bay. If there had not been so many ships going in and out of the Bay and blowing their horns at us (to ask us to get out of their way or to greet us?), we would have thought that we were at anchorage.

We finally reached open sea at night with Nojima Saki Light blinking farewell to us. I went on air and tuned my receiver to 8702kc. (We had been instructed to send all our messages to Taipei via JGC from now on instead of calling Keelung directly.) My 28th message went out like this:

CQ DE BEDM QSP TO 6056 TAIPEI NR28 CK15
171155GMT

ABEAM NOJIMA SAKI MAKING AHEAD SLOWLY
WITH E WIND 1 TO 2BS SEA SMOOTH OVERCAST

As soon as I keyed in the last letter, my receiver started clattering. The codes came over the air were so fast that all I could catch were scattered letters here and there that did not make any sense.

ST... MAR... MRES... STNDP... RESMERESUVMZSN... D...

I was too embarrassed to ask them to repeat. Finally I got something that I could recognize

BEDM DE JGC...

That was our call ID! But what followed immediately became jabbers again.

E... GSE... YOUR BROANGTST... ING... AD... ACI...

We had a long way to go yet. I wondered how was I going to keep contact with them from now on?

Eh, what the heck! After all, the communication had no purpose but for the papers to print news on our junk. Who cared?

XXIV

<u>June 18, 1955</u>

4,500 nautical miles to San Francisco

The sky was overcast. The sea was smooth. The junk was making 4 knots under a steady breeze. It was quiet on the poop deck. No shouting, no arguing, no talking, no excitement. The crew was engrossed in each one's own lingering land fever.

I was getting impatient to lose the lingering land sight. So I went into the cabin to hide myself in my Navigation/Radio corner, hoping that when I returned on deck the shoreline would have disappeared. I opened my logbook to draft a message for JGC to relay to Taipei. This was my 29th message since we left Keelung.

CQ DE BEDM QSP TO 6056 TAIPEI NR29 CK12

180755GMT

PSN 3440N 14031E WIND SE3 1012MB 24C OVERCAST

SEA LIGHT ALL WELL

As long as I could send out messages, I considered communication established. Whether I could take down the incoming messages or not was not important to me. They were mostly acknowledgments to my messages or requests we could not comply.

Cal came in to the Navigation/Radio Corner. He took a glance at the telegram I was going to send and said,

"Same message everyday? How dull! Listen, why don't you ask them to pass all your messages to the U.S. Navy Weather Center in Yokosuka?"

"Didn't you just say they were dull?"

"The ship's position was meaningful. Those people at the Weather Center may want to know it."

"Why should they be interested in our ship's position?"

"In case we had another disaster, they would know where to find us."

"Why do you think they want to find us? The General has already told us very clearly that once we got out to sea we would be on our own. In case of emergency, no one would come to our rescue."

"Well, as I told you before, there is an American tax payer on board."

These Americans, they thought being taxpayers they owned their country and being voters they ran their government.

"Why the weather center?"

"I know someone there."

"Male or female?"

True or not, there was no harm done to assume he was right. I changed my message to:

CQ DE BEDM QSP TO 6056 TAIPEI NR29 CK27
180755GMT
PSN 3440N 14031E WIND SE3 1012MB 24C OVERCAST
SEA LIGHT ALL WELL PSE PASS ALL OUR
INFORMATIONS FROM NOW ON TO US NAVY
WEATHER CENTER IN YOKOSUKA

June 19, 1955

4,350 nautical miles to San Francisco
Today's outgoing message (NR30) read like this:
CQ DE BEDM QSP TO 6056 TAIPEI NR30 CK10
190755GMT
PSN 3615N 14315E WIND S5 1004MB 22C SKY BLACK
SEA ROUGH

The shoreline finally submerged under the roaring sea that was hitting us constantly on our tack side. I could feel the blows on the rudder through the tiller in my hand. Now it would be a time to test our new shock absorbers. So far they seemed to work all right. No broken tiller. Animated talks returned to the poop deck.

The night was pitch dark. Everybody had turned in except

The Junk that Challenged the Yachts

Benny and I. I was on the tiller and Benny on the lookout watch. The wind had switched to E/N since midnight and we were following an E/N course. That meant we must sail close-hauled. We had been on starboard tack for quite a while. I decided to change tack. Benny went forward to take care of the sheets on the foresail. Just as I untied the leash on the tiller, Marco came out on deck.

"I'll take the tiller," he said to me while emptying his bladder over the side. I looked at him. He was half asleep in his sleeping long-john.

"I can handle it," I said

"I'll take over," he did not even button up his fly. "You go take care of the sheets."

Well, he was the captain. "Be my guest!" I said.

Although the wind was quite strong, on close-hauled the boat was not making too much speed. Instead of falling off down wind first to pick up some speed as I would do, Marco went straight into tacking by pushing the tiller hard a-lee. Then he put his foot on it like Washington crossing the Delaware River and watched the boat swinging into the wind.

The sails fluttered. The wind spilled out. The boat stalled. She failed to come about. Just then a huge wave with a white cap rolled in from our starboard side. It caught us broadside. The unleashed tiller shot out like a released cord on a tightened bow. I ducked.

A moment later as the boat eased up, I regained my foot stand. In front of my eyes was the tiller, springing back slowly without its handler. Where was Marco?

"Man overboard!" I yelled out in frenzy.

Benny rushed back from the foredeck. Half clothed bodies dashed out of the cabin: some went for the life buoy, some went for the ropes and someone threw a few bamboo poles over the side. Frantic voices filled the deck,

"Marco!"

"Marco!"

"Marco!"

There was no Marco.

I looked out to the water. It was dark like the navel of the Mother Earth. All I could see was the foam pushed out by the stalled junk while rolling with the waves. With the sheets still in my hands, I froze, watching the limping sheets lying loosely over the side where Marco had just disappeared. My mind went...

Suddenly I felt the sheets tightened up. With the fisherman's conditional reflex, I pulled the sheet in as if I was pulling on a fish line with a live swordfish on the hook. As the soaked rope slide over the side, I saw a hand, tightly holding onto the sheet.

"Marco!" I cried out.

June 20, 1955

4,260 nautical miles to San Francisco, Ship's Position 36°38'N 144°55'E, Temp 22°C

Despite the excitement we had the night before, we had a good sailing for several hours after changing tack.

Sailors were notorious in being vocal about the maltreatments they received from their captain. They would grab any opportunity to air their grievance. In menhaden fishing, for example, the crew cursed their captain through the laboring songs they sang when they were pulling in the net. On this junk, Marco had to listen to his crew's scolding after he got knocked overboard. It was like pouring vinegar on the bruises and cuts on his aching body.

"How much more stupid can a person be?" Huloo was the oldest among the crew. After he started it, everyone joined in.

"You want to hold off the ocean with your body? How big do you think you are?"

"Use your head instead of your body, Marco!"

"We could have lost you if the boat had succeeded in coming about."

"Do you know how long it would take us to turn this junk around? By the time we got back to where you fell in, you would have long been swallowed by those monstrous seas."

"Losing the captain to the sea on the third day out? You know what those people back home would say?"

"Why didn't you tie the tiller down when you tacked as we all do?"

"You behaved just like a landlubber!"

Marco took the insults without uttering one single word. That was exactly why he was elected the captain. Anyone else would have blown up.

For the rest of the day, Marco remained to be the topic of our talk.

June 21, 1955

4160 nautical miles to San Francisco, Ship's Position 37°03'N 146°42'E, Wind SW 3 B.S., Temp 24°C, Overcast, Sea light

We received a storm warning today:

PARA CYCLONE 998MBS AT 48N 156E

OFF KAMCHATKA MOVING EAST 20 KNTS

The cyclone was not threatening to us. It was northeast of us and moving away from us. If it had any effect on us at all, it could only give us some strong wind for sailing. So I redrew our course to get higher in the latitude. Perhaps I still had time to catch the tail of that cyclone.

"Is that a Great Circle course?" Cal asked as he watched me drawing the new course on the sailing chart.

"No."

"What is a Great Circle course?"

"It's the arc on the surface of the globe made by the plane that cuts through the center of the globe and the two points we are interested in, our ship's position and our destination," I explained. "It gives the shortest distance between these two points."

"If it is the shortest distance, why are we not sailing on a Great Circle course then?"

"On fishing boat, we are after the fish. On sailboat, we are after the wind. If there is no wind, what does distance mean? There is a prevailing westerly in the 43rd parallel. That is where we are heading for. It just happened that it is also where the cyclone is now."

However, to get there we must stay in the main shipping lane for a while.

<u>June 22, 1955</u>

4,040 nautical miles to San Francisco

I sent out another boring message (according to Cal's description):

CQ DE BEDM QSP 6056 TAIPEI NR35 CK12 221155GMT
PSN 3744N 14948E 1014MB 21C WIND WSW3
SEA MODERATE CLEAR ALL WELL

The wind direction had been rotating clockwise, from a strong southerly to a moderate westerly. That told me that I had caught the tail of the cyclone. We had some good sailing. But not for long, it tapered off after a few hours. We were becalmed. Not too long afterward, a heavy fog set in. We became not only crippled but also blind.

We got our foghorn out of the hold and cranked it at a regular interval. The fog was so thick that it condensed on my face and ran off my nose in a stream. The situation lasted all day into the night.

Shortly after midnight we heard a faint sound. It was a ship's horn. It came through the fog at a regular interval. It became louder and louder. Clearly the blower did not hear us. Since we had no way to get out of her way, Benny took out our pots and pans and started beating on them, hoping that a different sound might travel better on the water surface.

As the blasts got still louder, I took out the signal light and flashed it on the foresail, hoping that the spread of a white canvas could be more visible through the fog. Not knowing the code for BECALMED, I flashed the signal for DISABLED. But the blasting of the ship's horn indicated that she had neither seen us nor heard us. She kept heading toward us in a steady collision course. I called all hands on deck. The crew yelled and pounded on anything that would make a sound.

Then came the sound of a propeller slowly churning the water. That scared the daylight out of us. But we still could not see a thing. We couldn't even see our own bow. It wouldn't help even if we could see her. It was dead calm. We could not move.

"Get the life raft!" Marco yelled out. "Don't just stand there!

Pump it up!"

"Where is the pump?"

"Never mind. Go untie the sampan and the bamboo poles!"

"Cut them! No time to untie."

Just then came a long loud blast, as if it were blowing right next to my ear. I waited for the ominous moment.

The propeller suddenly sped up. In less than a minute, it faded out. The churning sound of the propeller was taken over by the ship's horn, blowing at the regular interval that we had first heard. We listened to it in awe until it totally disappeared into the fog.

We must get out of this shipping lane as quick as possible. But where is the wind?

June 23, 1955

3,930 nautical miles to San Francisco

CQ DE BEDM QSP 6056 TAIPEI NR37 CK12 231155GMT PSN 3842N 15125E WIND N/E3 16C PARTLY CLOUDY SEA MODERATE SPEED 3KNTS

After breakfast Benny went down to the hold to carry out his daily routine in pumping the bilge and charging the batteries. Less than a minute later he was back on deck, breathless.

"There is a leak!" he said.

"How bad?" alarming voices filled the cabin.

"Half an inch in the bilge from yesterday to this morning."

"Did you taste it?"

"Not salty if that's what you mean."

"Whew, I thought the sky was going to fall down," said Marco in relief. "At least the boat is not leaking. It's just the water tanks. Let's find the leak after breakfast and have it plugged up."

"It tasted sour."

That got everybody nervous again. We quickly drew some water out to taste. We found that it had a deep red color. We tried the other tanks. They were all the same.

Thank God the water in the original tank under the galley was good. That was the tank the former crew used their coastal sailing. But we had to cover 4,600 miles!

We measured the compartment. It measured 4' deep, 12' beam and 3' wide. When multiplied by 75% to account for the curved shape of the hull, we got 800 gallons. Assuming each person consumed one gallon per day, that would last us for 133 days.

A water ration was immediately implemented.

"No water is to be wasted," said the captain. "Every drop of water expended from now on must be swallowed down your throat. That means no brushing of teeth and no rinsing of rice with fresh water."

"It's all Hsiao Chow's crazy idea of building those water tanks," Huloo complained. "We shouldn't have listened to him. We should have filled all the cargo holds with fresh water instead. Like the American Seaplane-tender captain told us, our bulkheads are all watertight. As a matter of fact, the one we are now using was converted from one of those holds. That way we would not only have ballast and all the fresh water we want to waste but also have saved lots of money. The holds were used to load salt fish. So the water might smell fishy. But who cares?"

"If you are so smart, why didn't you mention it earlier?" I retorted.

"It's your junk and your money to throw away."

"You still claim you can solo on this trip?"

"Why not?"

"Not having anybody to blame, you would be bored to death."

"Stop your silly argument on your nostalgia!" Marco broke in to stop us. "Let's face an urgent problem. Shall we drain the tanks?" he asked.

"No," more than one voice cried out in unison. Fresh water was fresh water. At sea it was the most precious thing, colored or sour. In case of emergency, it was better than none. Besides, now without the rocks, we needed it for ballast.

Actually Huloo's idea of filling up the holds for ballast purpose would not work. When the vessel rolled, the water would rush to the low side and make the vessel list more. We could even capsize. But I did not want to bring it up. If he were proven wrong, he would certainly pick on me for something else.

June 24, 1955
 3900 nautical miles to San Francisco
 CQ DE BEDM QSP 6056 TAIPEI NR38 CK8 241155GMT
 PSN 3920N 15200E WIND S2 17C ALL WELL
 Slow sailing. Another boring day. Another boring message. Cal raised another question.

 "Did you report Marco's incident to Taipei?"

 "No."

 "Why not? This is the kind of news the newspaper are dying for."

 "You want me to make Marco's sister lose her sleep and appetite again?"

 "Why would she lose her sleep? It's a happy ending after all."

 "You don't know Chinese women. They can dwell on the scary part of an event for a long time. She could go crazy by imagining what worse things could have happened even though it never happened."

 "Then don't mention Marco's name. Just say a crew member."

 "Then you make more women sleepless."

 "Say it was me."

 "Then it'll bring all the girls on the Chungking Victory into tears."

 "What about our encountering with the ship in the fog? Did you report it?"

 "What ship?"

 "That ship we met couple of days ago."

 "Did you see it?"

 "No, but we all heard her."

 "Then it must be a ghost ship. There is nothing to report about a ghost ship."

 "Say it's a sea serpent."

 "Go away!"

 Cal threw up his hands and said, "I don't understand at all how you Chinese think. No humor. No imagination."

June 25, 1955

    CQ DE BEDM QSP 6056 TAIPEI NR39 CK16
    PSN 4015N 15356E 1008MB 17C WIND NW3
    OCCASIONAL RAIN VISIBILITY POOR
    SQUALL AT 2202GMT ALL WELLS

I noticed that recently Cal had been sleeping late in the mornings and missing the breakfast. I was on watch this morning when he finally got up after all the pots and bowls had been cleaned. He brushed his teeth.

"Is that fresh water?" I asked in suspicion.

"It's my portion of water in the *shee-fan* that I skipped this morning," he said. *Shee-fan* was the watery rice porridge that the Chinese served in all their breakfasts.

"That does not matter," I said in a stern voice. "Fresh water is fresh water. It must be swallowed down your throat as the captain has ordered whether you ate your *shee-fan* or not."

After rinsing his mouth, he swallowed the water.

"Are you satisfied now?" he asked me in sarcasm. Then he went down to the hold. A little while later he came up with a can of peaches from the batch of canned food given to us by Gen. Chase of MAAG. He opened it and offered some to me. It looked awfully tempting. But I refused. I was going to say, "All the provisions on board are to be shared by the entire crew regardless of to whom they were given. No individual serving." But I thought I had already given him enough hard time on the fresh water. I shouldn't be too harsh on him. In fact, I had never seen a single foreigner to like the Chinese *shee-fan*. When Cal told us that he could have rice every meal, I guessed *shee-fan* did not cross his mind or he had never tasted any before.

June 26, 1955

    CQ DE BEDM QSP 6056 TAIPEI NR40 CK18 260755GMT
    PSN 4007N 15554E 1012MB 13C BEATING AGAINST
    COLD WIND NE4 OVERCAST OCCASIONAL RAIN
    VISIBILITY POOR SQUALL AT 2202GMT

The Junk that Challenged the Yachts

The cold on North Pacific was not like the biting winter cold on the Yellow Sea. It would not cut open your skin. It penetrated your body and got right to your bones. The only way to escape it was to get into your bunk and read. But since I was a kid, I never liked reading.

Cal occupied the bunk above mine. Every time he climbed into his bunk, he had to use mine as a step.

"Who's that girl?" he pointed to the picture pinned on the bulkhead right next to my pillow. The guy was so nosy, I thought. He must have wanted to ask that question for a long time. I just ignored him.

"His cousin," Reno answered for me.

"Too pretty for a cousin," Cal said. "You know what we call that in America? A kissing cousin."

"It is her cousin," Benny confirmed in all seriousness.

"Oh, you Chinese. All the boys call their girlfriends little sisters and the girls calls their boyfriends big brothers."

"Doesn't that sound better than honey and sugar?" Huloo added his comment.

June 27, 1955

3,650 nautical miles to San Francisco
CQ DE BEDM QSP 6056 TAIPEI NR41 CK11 271155GMT
PSN 4005N 15904E 1022MB 12C WIND N2 OVERCAST
MAKING LITTLE HEADWAY

I got a headache from staying too long in my bunk. That was where I had spent all my time recently except my eight-hour-per-day watch and the radio communication session. My junk mates recommended a book for me to read, a translation of Monte Christo. It supposed to be a suspense story. But I had to put it down several times in just the first hour. I looked around the cabin. Marco was sound asleep; Reno was reading; Cal was sitting up in his bunk typing. I wonder what were really going through their heads. I forced myself back to my reading.

June 28, 1955

CQ DE BEDM QSP 6056 TAIPEI NR42 CK15 281155GMT
PSN 4007N 15950E 1025MB 13C NO WIND ALL SAILS
DOWN CHECK RIGGING REPLACE WORN ROPES

"Listen," Cal said to me after he got down from the mast. Huloo had sent him up to slush the mast. "If we keep sending these dry messages day after day, pretty soon no newspaper will want to print them. In no time the *Free China* will disappear in the Pacific like Richard Halliburton."

"Who's Richard Halliburton?"

"He was an adventure writer. Back in 1935, he had a Chinese junk built in Hong Kong to sail cross the Pacific and to enter the Golden Gate Bridge on the opening day of the World's Fair in San Francisco. He never made it. He simply disappeared in the Pacific. To this day no one can figure out what has happened to him."

"The trouble is he had a new junk, never been tested. It would never happen to us. An old junk like ours would have survived many many storms and typhoons."

"I did not mean sinking literally. I mean disappearing from the public. We got to give the press something more exciting to report."

"If there were something exciting, I would like to hear it first," Reno joined in. "Life is so boring on this boat!"

"I have an idea."

"What?"

"Our next message should read like this: *Rough sea. Mainsail stuck in dousing. American sent aloft to slush mast. He fell...*"

"Then what?"

"Then we wait. The news will take care of itself."

"How?"

"It will immediately get from the last page back to the front page on every newspaper."

"But you did not fall!"

"That can be arranged. I'll just climb back up on the mast and then jump into the water. I need a bath anyway."

"That is called acting. Besides, we don't want to go through the trouble in fishing you out."

"I can swim. Look, there's not even a breeze."

"It can kick up at anytime. Remember last time you went for a swim?"

"I'll just jump in and climb back up right away."

"You do that. But if I don't send the message, you won't have a story."

"Forget it. I'm just trying to help out."

June 29, 1955

Ship's Position 40°31'N 160°28'E, Wind SSW 3 B.S.,

Temp 14°C, Overcast, Sea light

The wind picked up at dusk. Around midnight, it became so strong that our mainsail was torn at its leech. One batten broke. We had to reduce the sail to half sail.

June 30, 1955

Ship's Position 41°20'N 164°17'E, Wind WNW 4 B.S.,

Temp 10°C, Overcast, Sea rough

The tiller broke at 9 am. Good thing we had made a lot of spares in Yokosuka. We put in a new tiller and lowered the mainsail further to one third and the foresail all the way down. That took a lot of strain off the tiller.

July 1, 1955

Ship's Position 41°15'N 166°25'E, Wind NNW 6 B.S.,

Temp 10°C, Overcast, Sea very rough

Sailing at 6 knots all day with one-third mainsail and no foresail. The second tiller broke. We realized that we could not depend totally on the shock absorbers to take the shocks. We went back to our old practice, namely easing off the leash every time the sea hit. The lesson learned: Nothing on this old junk is absolutely dependable, including the traditional junk seamanship.

July 2, 1955

Ship's Position 39°58'N 167°48'E, Wind ENE 1 B.S.,

Temp 12°C

The breeze could barely stir the flag that was hung above the poop deck. The junk ran out of wind to move and we ran out of topics to argue.

"I smell something rotten inside the cabin," Huloo broke the silence.

Now that he had mentioned it, we all could smell it.

"Dead rat!"

That immediately set off a search for dead rats. At the end of the day, no dead rat was found.

<u>July 3, 1955</u>

Ship's Position 41°56'N 168°14'E, Wind E/N 2 B.S.,
Temp 11°C

We finally found out where the rotten smell came from. We found a pile of fermented rice in the bilge. It was traced to a hole on a rice sack. Rats! They must be the perpetrators! We must catch them.

Huloo made a cage with bamboo strips from our broken battens. "We'll have some fresh meat to eat for a change," he said.

"Very expensive meat," Reno added. "Fed on good white rice, not to mention that which has leaked out to the bilge."

"You know, we can make wine from fermented rice."

"You know how to do it?" Marco was elated to hear that.

"Of course."

"Then make some."

"I don't have yeast."

"Use that fermented rice in the bilge."

"You had already thrown it overboard."

<u>July 4, 1955</u>

Ship's Position 42°50'N 169°10'E, Wind SSE 2 B.S.,
Temp 13°C

Marco asked me to send a telegram to his sister:

CQ DE BEDM QSP 6056 TAIPEI NR49 CK16 041155GMT
PSN 4250N 16910E 1027MB 13C SSE2
TO MRS DAVID FONG 1 LANE 16 SECTION 2 HO PING

WEST ROAD TAIPEI HAPPY BIRTHDAY WE ALL WELL
LOVE TO MARY CHUNG

"Why did you address your sister as Mrs. Fong?" Reno asked.
"Isn't she a Chung?"

"She is married to the Fong family."

"Since when did the Chinese women go by their husbands'
family name?"

"Since Hsiao Chow is using English in his radio message. In
English language, do as English do."

"Eh, you foreigner worshipper!"

Mary was Marco's girlfriend. They met through the old
Chinese way, match making. A few years ago Marco was sent to
Thailand on an official trip. There was no direct flight between
Taiwan and Thailand. He had to make a change in Hong Kong. So
the matchmaker asked him to bring a sweater to a girl who was a
music teacher in Hong Kong. Marco never got to give the sweater
to the girl. He gave it to her uncle, who was her guardian. He saw
the girl but never talked to her because the uncle was doing all the
talking to check out the suitor. When he returned to Taiwan, with
the girl's guardian's approval of course, Marco started writing to
her. On the junk there was no postal service. So he entered a page a
day in a bound notebook.

"Life is so boring on this junk," Reno said to Marco. "What
do you find to be so interesting that you can write about every day?
You are not just repeating the same thing like Napoleon did to
Josephine on the battlefield, '*I hold you in my arms and in my
heart every day and every night*', are you?"

"There is a lot to write about in our life if you put your heart
to it."

"Read us something that you have written."

Without hesitation, he read us what he had just written today:

"Mary, do you know what day it is today? It's my brother-in-
law's birthday. We had noodles for lunch, not for David but for
America. It's also America's birthday. Cal wanted to document his
patriotism in motion picture, to show it to his boss I guess. He
made a sign in English saying July Fourth, 1955 and something

like happy birthday. We thought he should say *America Ten Thousand Years* like we do in Chinese. He said that would not be American. We asked him what is American. He said American flag (which we don't have), apple pie (which we don't know what he is talking about without having tasted one) and fireworks (that we do know). When Reno was shooting a scene on Cal longing for his homeland with his movie camera, I sneaked a pack of firecrackers under his pants. You should have seen the way he jumped up. He couldn't complain because, as he said, firework was American. In fact, he liked it so much that he asked Reno to do another take. Luckily I had picked up a lot of leftover firecrackers from the parting party they gave us on our first departure. By the way, everyone liked my noodles. I'll make it for you everyday after we get married."

"When did you propose to her?"

"I never did."

"How do you know she will marry you?"

"She will."

"That word LOVE in your telegram does not sound very Chinese."

"I know. Cal talked me into using it."

"You think she would approve it?"

"It would for sure give her goose bumps."

<u>July 5, 1955</u>

Ship's Position 43°02'N 171°10'E, Wind SSE 2 B.S.,

Temp 14°C, Sea smooth

When Cal asked his boss for a leave to come on this trip, he told them that, being the sole foreigner on board, he would have a unique opportunity to learn Chinese "by immersion". When he came on board, he made good to his promise. He had been learning ten new Chinese words every day. His mentor was Marco.

"What got you interested in learning Chinese?" Marco asked him.

"I don't know."

"Chinese girls?"

"Perhaps."

"How are they different from American girls?"

"You mean Western girls. They are all Americans. The Oriental girls have less hair on their arms than the Western girls."

"Are you speaking from experience?"

"Of course."

"Any particular girl?"

"There was this one I went to college with at Berkeley."

"What's her name?"

"Isadora."

"Does she know you are interested in her?"

"I don't know. But she said in her last letter I received in Japan through our mutual college friend, Alex Mayeda, 'Look out for two little feet bearing six towels at the dock when you arrive in San Francisco.' What do you make of that?"

July 6, 1955

Ship's Position 43°20'N 173°10'E, Wind S 2 B.S.,

Temp 13°C, Foggy

I came on watch as the dawn was barely breaking. The fog had disbursed. But there was still a mist hanging around. The moon was peeking out of the clouds from time to time. Benny was hanging on the tiller by an arm. Not a word was heard from him. His eyebrows were dripping with dew. His pupils were twinkling with the reflections of the moon. His mind was somewhere else.

He suddenly noticed my presence. He fumbled his hand in his pocket for a while and pulled out a piece of paper. He handed it to me and said, "This is what I wrote an hour ago."

East pale
Waning moon hangs on sail's tip.
Light rain fades
Cloud and mist collect
Chilly breeze sweeps blue ripples
Little boat has her day.

"It's beautiful. I can even feel it," I said. "Are you going to send it to your girlfriend?"

"I don't have a girlfriend."

"Then are you going to send it to your principal's daughter?"

"I'll think about it."

July 7, 1955

Ship's Position 43°30'N 175°56'E, Wind SSW 4 B.S.,

Temp 14°C, Fog lasted 56 hours

Cal like Benny's poem so much that he translated it into English:

The ocean's dark night yields to dawn's glow

While a waning moon peers over the sail's edge.

Nocturnal mists surrender to clearing skies

As a chill breeze ruffles the dark blue sea.

A small boat rolls along a lonely pathway into the dawn.

Benny was a scholar in Chinese. Although he did not know any English, he strongly believed that poems could not be translated from one language to another. He qualified his belief to Cal by saying, "I have read several translations of Shakespeare. They all sounded awful, harsh to my ears. But I'm sure they sound beautiful in English. You see, once translated, they lost all their touches and feelings, which are all what poetry is about. The Chinese poems, for example, are songs. If you cannot sing them, then they are no good. They have beats."

"Like the beat in music?" Cal asked.

"Not quite. The Chinese beat in poem goes with tones in words. Take this Li Po poem for instance, *Chuang qian ming yue guang...*" Benny recited with a heavy Cantonese accent. "You know that one?"

"Yes, *Chuang qian ming yue guang,*" Cal repeated it in Mandarin and then translated it into his own language. "*The moonlight in front of my window.*"

"Now sing it."

"*Chuang qian ming yue guang,*" Cal sang in a tune that he just made up ad hoc.

"Do you feel the awkwardness?"

"No."

"But the beat is wrong. You see, the beat Li Po wrote the poem in is:

"*Tze, tze, tze, tze, ping. Tze* is second tone, which applies to the first four words in that line. *Ping* is first tone, which applies only to the last word. But the first word you sang was in the first tone, a *ping*. It definitely does not belong there."

"How do you know the correct beat is not *Ping, tze, tze, tze, ping?*"

"Ah, you are talking like a Chinese poet. What is the second verse of that poem?"

"*Yi shi di shang shuang.*"

"Very good. *Is mistaken as frost on the ground.* Now tell me what is the beat for the second verse?"

"*Tze, tze, tze, tze, ping.*"

"Very good! So?"

"So the beat for the first verse must also be *Tze, tze, tze, tze, ping.* You mean Li Po made a booboo?"

"No, you made a booboo. In fact most people has made this booboo. The first word should not be *WINDOW*. It should be *BED*. Both *BED* and WINDOW are pronounced *CHUANG*. But *BED* is pronounced in the second tone that fit in with the beat: *tze, tze, tze, tze, ping.*"

"No wonder in San Francisco people call the Chinese language the singsong Chinese."

"It's not a joking matter. We do sing. In fact, you can sing better in the literary Cantonese than in the barbaric Mandarin. We have seven tones and they have only four tones." Then he sang out in his Cantonese dialect:

"The moonlight in front of my bed
Is mistaken as frost on the ground."

July 8, 1955

We were still in the Eastern Hemisphere, Ship's Position 43°45'N 178°45'E, Wind SSW 4 B.S., Temp 13C 1020MB Sea rough, Good sailing. We made 178 miles during the last 24 hours.

"Do you really think I should send my poem to Miss. Yao?"

Benny asked me when I came onto the poop deck. He and Cal were on watch. He was on the tiller.

"Yes," I said.

"Can you take over the tiller, Cal?" Benny said to Cal. Then without saying another word he went into the cabin. A little while later he came back on deck with a whisky bottle that Marco and Inspector Lo had emptied in Okinawa. He took out from his pocket the paper he had showed me on the previous day. He wrote something on it and stuck it into the bottle. After spending half an hour in sealing it with lead wrapper and wax, he threw it overboard.

"You think she will get it?" I asked.

"That's the only mail service available at sea. Why are you throwing out those current testing bottles everyday?"

"There are so many of them. Some of them will be picked up by some beachcombers for sure. You have only one bottle. Perhaps you should throw in a few empty bottles to increase the chance of your bottle being picked up."

"Nonsense!" Reno broke in our conversation. He just came on deck to replace Benny on the watch. "Everything has its own destiny. The chance of a particular bottle of yours for being picked up does not depend on the chances of all the other bottles for not being picked up. If you had thrown into the sea just that one bottle which will be picked up and not the others, it will still be picked up by the same beachcomber. It's the same way with people's fortune. My fortune does not depend on your fortune. In other words, the chance of that beachcomber to pick up that bottle does not depend on the chances of all those other beachcombers to miss the other bottles."

Come to think of it, Reno's got a point. But I had to think about it more to be convinced.

We had been sailing in fog for the last 80 hours at various speeds. As soon as it got dark, we shortened our sails. We were still making 6 knots on a beam reach.

Reno was on the tiller and Marco was afore on the lookout when I came back on deck at 10pm.

"What is that?" pointing to the wooden box I had in my hands, Reno asked.

"My brother's ashes," I said.

"Why do you bring it on deck?"

"We are going to cross the 180th meridian soon."

"What does that have to do with your brother's ashes?"

"My brother had always wanted to go to sea. So he came to Taiwan with me. But he died too soon. He was only nineteen. I have kept his ashes all these years while looking for a place to bury him. I think the sea is the most suitable place. After all, he was killed at sea so to speak. I'll scatter his ashes at the 180th meridian so that he could reach both halves of the globe."

"I don't think that's a good idea."

"He loved the sea. When he was back home in Tsingtao, he spent most of his summer on the beach and in the water."

"Did you ask your mother about this?"

"Why ask my mother?"

"He's more of your mother's son than of your brother."

"How can I ask her? She is in Shanghai and I am here."

"Then you should wait until you see her."

"My brother would have come with us on this trip if he were alive."

"He is now with you. And you want to throw him overboard? Don't you want him to complete the trip with you?"

Reno talked as if my brother were alive. I had never known him to be so sentimental. I only knew him as a fatalist, a gambler and a fun-seeker.

We crossed the 180th meridian at ten minutes after midnight. I did not throw the box overboard. I took it into the cabin and put it back at the head of my bunk.

July 8, 1955

We were now in the Western Hemisphere, 2,550 nautical miles to San Francisco, Ship's Position 43°03'N 178°50'W, Wind NNW 1 B.S., Temp 13°C, Fog lasted for 80 hours

We had made 110 nautical miles during the past 24 hours.

"Hey, Reno, you know so many girls. Do you have one that you are serious with?" Cal asked Reno.

"Neh."

"Seriously."

"Eh."

"Is she tall?"

"No."

"Is she pretty?"

"Hey, hey, hey, hey..."

"Is she a gambler?"

"No. But in betting on me, I guess she has to be a gambler."

"She like movie?"

"Not as much as I do."

"What kind of music she likes?"

"Anything I listen to."

"She reads?"

"Never asked her. But whatever I tried to tell her, she already knew."

"She goes out with other boys?"

"How would I know?"

"I got the picture," said Cal. Then he stopped asking more questions.

July 9, 1955

2,530 nautical miles to San Francisco, Ship's Position 42°45'N 178°28'W, Wind nil, Temp 13°C, Becalmed 40 hours, Transmitter No. 2 out of order

Counting the extra day we gained on July 8 by crossing the 180th meridian, we had been at sea for 23 days and we were 250 miles short of half way to our destination. With this averaged speed, we should be in San Francisco on August 9. If we wanted to match Folster's record, we had to do much better than this.

"Everyone start to pray for more wind," ordered the captain.

"Are there any Christians or Buddhists among us?" Cal asked.

"It doesn't matter," said Reno. "If we are destined to have winds, we will have them whether we pray or not."

July 10, 1955

2,530 nautical miles to San Francisco, Ship's Position 43°05'N 178°00'W, Wind E/N 4 B.S., Temp 13°C

We finally got some wind after being becalmed for more than 50 hours. But it was in the adverse direction. We had to tack. I tied my dirty clothes on a heaving line and threw them over the stern.

"What are you doing that for?" Cal asked.

"To have my clothes washed."

"Hey, it's like a washing machine!"

"Washing machine?"

"In America we wash our clothes in washing machines."

"In China our clothes are hand-washed."

"Who does the hand-washing for you?"

"Washing maids."

"Who washes for your washing maids?"

I was stunned speechless by Cal's question. Who washed for the washing maids? I had never given any thought to it.

"I see you are not a typical Chinese," Cal said.

"Uh?"

"People like your washing maids constitute 90% of the Chinese population. They are the typical Chinese. Intellectuals like you make up less than 10%. Whatever you claim the Chinese do is not even known to the average Chinese. It is known only to you guys. To the *Chinese,* you intellectuals are just as foreign as I am."

"We are not intellectuals. We are fishermen. We are what you called the proletariats."

"Proletariats my foot. Your parents were educated in America; Huloo's and Reno's fathers worked as engineers in an American telephone company; Marco's father is a manager in an American hospital; Benny's grandfather owned tens of fishing boats. You call them proletariats? You call that typical Chinese? I doubt if any of you know how a typical Chinese live and work. You told me while you were fishing on the China Coast, you were fishing among many junks. Do you know what their lives were like, what they wore, what they ate and what they were thinking? You told me you

140

had saved $800 in your nine years of fishing. Do you know what a junk fisherman has saved in his entire life? By the way, how many of their fish lines have your America diesel boat cut through? Have you ever given a thought to how much it would cost for them to replace them?"

It had never crossed my mind.

July 11, 1955

Ship's Position 42°45'N 177°15'W

So far I had been taking only sun sights and evening star sights for determining our ship's positions. It would be nice if I could also take some star sights. To do that, I must be able to see the horizon. But my sexton was not equipped with a bubble-level to give me an artificial horizon at night. Tonight the sky was exceptionally clear and the sea was smooth. It was full of stars. One could see them all the way down to the skyline. That gave me an idea. Wasn't the bright star-filled skyline the horizon? I climbed up onto the fantail with my sextant to try out the idea. While struggling to see the "horizon", I overheard the conversation between Reno and Cal.

"This reminds me of the night in the Sierra," Cal said.

"Where is Sierra?" Reno asked.

"A high mountain range in California."

"How the hell could the sea remind you of a mountain?"

"They are both under a sky full of stars."

"What were you doing on the mountain?"

"Hiking."

"At night?"

"We hiked during the day and camped out at night."

"You must be crazy. Why on earth did you do that for?"

"To be out in the nature. Don't the Chinese hike?"

"We hike all the time, running away from the Japanese during the war and going to work and going to the market at peace time."

"I mean out in the wilderness, no electricity, no running water no toilet."

"All our villages are like that, no electricity, no running water, no toilet."

"I mean for you city people."

"Most of us have spent some time in the villages at one time or another during the war to get out of harm's way of the Japanese soldiers. It's hardship. Why do we want to do that for leisure?"

"What do you do for leisure?"

"Going to movies."

"I mean exercise."

"We pull nets, move fish boxes and shovel ice. What do you do for exercise?"

"I run."

"Run like what a rickshaw man does?"

"Yes, but without a rickshaw or anything, not even a partner, so that I can run anywhere and anytime."

"How did you pick that boring thing as an exercise?"

"It's not boring at all, not like life on this junk. With two legs you can run to any place you want. My brother runs. He is a record holder of a two-mile course."

"What's his name?"

"Charlie."

"Will we meet him?"

"You bet your life."

"I bet with money, cigarettes, never with my life."

July 12, 1955

Ship's Position 43°26'N 176°00'W, Temp 15°C, Easterly wind mostly for the past three days.

"Tell me, the fellow I replaced, what is he like?" Cal asked me this morning.

"Lin Fung-Chu is a young fisherman who is not mature enough even to have his own opinion. He is vulnerable and listens to everybody's advice readily. That was how we recruited him and how we lost him. We asked him if he wanted to join us, he immediately said yes. Later when the older fishermen told him that it was dangerous, he immediately had cold feet. He could never..."

"I don't mean Lin. I've met him. I mean the one before him."

"Oh, Chiang, Huai-Ren. His father is the Chinese ambassador to the United Nations."

"Remember what I said yesterday?" Cal reminded me. "You are all the elites of China."

I was not in the mood to carry on an old argument with him. So I went on,

"He was a junior engineering officer on a Navy ship before joining the fishing fleet. Before that, he went to a boarding school, Holy Light High School in Chungking, where my mother was the dean of students. Once he was brought to my mother by the school security guard for trying to sneak out of the campus during the study period in the evening. My mother took out a ruler and asked him to drop his pants. He refused. That brought the English pastor into the picture. He told my mother, 'Yes, they do cane pupils in England, but not a sixteen-year-old boy on his bare bottom.' My mother retorted in saying, 'Why not? I still spank my 17-year-old and 18-year-old boys on their bare bottoms.'"

Cal broke out laughing. He finally got hold of himself and said to me,

"That proved two of my points. One, the Chinese education was run by foreigners, in this case an English pastor and an American educated dean in a missionary school. Two, the Chinese circle you belong to, the elites, is so small that you can all relate to one another, Chiang to your mother and later you to Chiang. You are no typical Chinese."

July 13, 1955

Ship's Position 43°25'N 173°46'W, Wind S 3 B.S., Temp 17°C
Got in touch with KSF at 8558 kc. Last message to JGC:
JGC DE BEDM
GOT CONTACT WITH KFS AT 1455 GMT ALL WELL COMPLIMENTS AND THANKS TO JGC MEMBERS FROM THE FREE CHINA CREW PSE TELL CHINESE CONSULATE GENERAL ABOUT THIS

July 14, 1955

    Ship's Position 43°05'N 171°00'W, Wind E/N 4 B.S.,
Temp 13°C, Becalmed 40 hours
Calvin asked me to send a telegram for him:
KFS DE BEDM NR59 CK45 JUNK FREE CHINA
COLLECT 150755GMT NRT
DEPARTMENT OF STATE WASHINGTON DC MID
PACIFIC REPORT JUNK FREE CHINA POSITION 43N
171W CREW EXCELLENT SPIRITS HEALTH ADVERSE
WEATHER HAS SLOWED SAILING BUT NOW MAKING
5 KNOTS AVERAGE ETA SAN FRANCISCO EARLY
AUGUST CHINESE STUDIES PROGRESSING PLEASE
EXTEND LWOP TO AUGUST 15 RESPCETFULLY
MEHLERT

    "What is LWOP?" I asked him after I had received an acknowledgment from KFS.

    "Leave Without Pay."

    "How stingy your government is! We quit our jobs before coming on this trip. But they did not stop our pay."

    "Why?"

    "They wanted us to go back."

    "How much is your pay?"

    "Benny and I get equivalent to $20 a month. Marco, Huloo and Paul get $40 because they were all in charge of something. If your government is not paying you, why do you need to ask them for an extension?"

    "They let me come because they figured I could learn more Chinese from you guys."

    "They'll be pretty disappointed when they find you speaking like a fisherman."

    "Guan ta-ma-de!" Cal expressed in his favorite three-character profanity.

July 15, 1955

    Ship's Position 42°16'N 168°12'W, Wind S 3 B.S.,
Temp 17°C, Heavy fog, Speed 4 knots

Since both Marco and Cal had sent personal telegrams, I thought I should also send a message to my uncle and aunt to thank them for depositing $500 for each of us in an American bank as required by the American vice consul in charge of the visa section, my own shipmate Calvin Mehlert:

KFS DE BEDM

NR.60 CK28 JUNK FREE CHINA COLLECT 160755GMT NRT

MR AND MRS PAO G SHEN 131 NEW MARKET ROAD GARDEN CITY NY LOVE FROM MID PACIFIC 2000 MILES FROM SAN FRANCISCO DREAMING OF AUNTS GOOD COOKING PAUL

"You didn't say thank you," noticed Cal.

"I did say that I was dreaming of my aunt's good cooking, didn't I?" I pointed out to him. "The word THANK-YOU is too awkward to say among close relatives and acquaintances."

"But you used LOVE. Wouldn't it sound more awkward to the Chinese ears?"

"Sure, it sounds sissy to say it to a young girl. But it's all right to say it to an elder."

July 16, 1955

Ship's Position 43°21'N 165°26'W, Wind S 3 B.S., Temp 17°C, 30 days at sea. 2,550 miles covered. 2,100 miles to go.

The Americans were quite different from the Japanese. I could tell from Morse Code. After having made contact with KFS for just three days, we already got into the habit of chitchatting before sending our messages. Today the operator asked for my name. Then he gave me his. From then on we were on first name basis.

We had been making an average of 100 miles per day lately. If the wind would keep up like this, we would still be able to beat Folster's record of 48 days.

July 17, 1955

Ship's Position 43°26'N 163°40'W, Wind SSE 1 B.S.,

Temp 15°C

I had said it too early. The wind was barely enough to keep the sail from swinging from side to side. Got nothing much to do in such a slow sailing. So we renewed all the chafed ropes in the rigging.

July 18, 1955

Ship's Position 43°43'N 162°17'W, Wind E 3 B.S., Temp 16°C, Speed 3 knots

The wind picked up just as we had all the rigging replaced. We had nothing else to do except to contemplate that we had 1830 more miles to sail. How many more days were there for us to be cooped up in these 500 square feet of cabin space and poop deck? To avoid getting into an argument was not that hard. To avoid talking to some one was hard. But Reno and Benny had not been talking to each other since we moved to live on board the junk except for absolute necessity. Actually I had noticed that since they came back from their treasure hunt.

They were captains on two purse seiners. After the mullet season, their boats were rented to some Japanese company to hunt for a Japanese wreck that was sunken by the Allies airplanes somewhere in the Taiwan Strait toward the end of World War II. Her cargo was the treasures the Japanese government had taken from China. While the Japanese were moving deep sea diving equipments on board, the crew rushed ashore to buy themselves some more detailed charts for the Strait. They thought if the Japanese ever came upon something, they would have to go back to rent some bigger vessel to retrieve the treasure. With every movement marked on the charts, the fishermen figured they could beat the Japanese back to it afterward because that was their neck of woods.

The operation was carried by the two fishing boats dragging a cable across the sea floor where the Japanese thought the ship had gone down. When the cable hooked on something, the boats would drop their anchors and the divers would go down to conduct a further investigation. It turned out that the boats' cable never

146

hooked on anything.

Ever since the two purse seiners returned to port, Reno and Benny stopped talking to each another. What had happened on their treasure hunt? When I tried to find out, all I got was a comment from Reno.

"Eh, the Japanese are very tricky. They were just trying to eliminate some of their doubts. You think they are that stupid to ask us to drag even near where they think the ship had gone down? Remember, we are Chinese."

What did that have to do with his not talking to Benny?

July 19, 1955

Ship's Position 45°03'N 160°05'W, Wind SE 3 B.S., Temp 15°C, Cloudy

Being professional fishermen for almost ten years, we thought if we could not do anything we could at least catch fish. We had been trying to catch some fish on this trip. We had a troll line on our stern all the time. So far all the fish we had seen were either the flying fish attracted by the deck light of our escort, MV Yu Hsiang, between Keelung and No Man Island or the mackerel given to us by the fish mongers in Yokosuka. In Tokyo we met a professor of fisheries who was keen on trolling. He made three troll baits for us. We had them trolled at different lengths of troll lines. None of them caught anything until this morning. One of them caught a big one. It was an albatross, a sea bird as big as a goose. After a heated debate in what to do with it, Huloo wrapped a copper band around its leg and let it go. On the band he carved the date and position it was caught and released.

"There goes a meal," said Reno. "When are we going to have the chicken, Huloo?"

Huloo just ignored him.

July 20, 1955

Ship's Position 45°27'N 158°55'W, Wind variable, Temp 16°C, Cloudy

I got off the watch at six in the morning and immediately

climbed into my bunk. Just as I fell asleep, Cal climbed over my bunk to get his movie camera. He woke me up excitedly, "Whales!"

I turned away from him and tried to get back to sleep.

But the commotion on deck kept me up. I was so mad in having my sleep interrupted for such trivial thing that I refused the temptation to get up. What's the big deal about whales? The ocean was full of them. So I missed this one. I would see another one.

"Look, there is another one!" voices in excitement on the poop deck kept streaming into the cabin through the open galley doorway.

"There is another one over there!"

"How do you know they are whales?"

"Look at the way they spray! Whales breathe through blowholes."

"How come they don't show their tails?"

"They don't have tails."

"Look, there is a whole flock of them coming at us."

"Will they collide with us?"

"It won't. That is just one big giant sea serpent showing several sections of its back."

"Not seeing the ends, they sure look like different sections of a long snake. It must be huge."

"Why do they hang around us?"

"Wow! That one almost touched us."

"What has kept them from bumping into us?"

"Why do they come so close?"

"They think we were one of them, a bigger brother, a sea serpent."

"Can't they see we have sails?"

"They can't see anything above water."

"Perhaps that's why they jump out of the water, to take a look at us."

I could not stay in my bunk any longer. I came on deck. There was nothing around us, just a smooth sea, no whale, no sea serpent, no nothing! The crew was engaged in a hot argument about the tails of whales, perpendicular or horizontal to their bodies. I joined in.

<u>July 21, 1955</u>
1,635 miles to San Francisco, Ship's Position 45°25'N 158°00'W, Wind N 1 B.S., Temp 16°C

For days I had had this feeling that I did not want to share with any of my shipmates. With nothing but all this water around me, I started to doubt if the land we tried to reach, or for that matter the land we last saw, was still there. How would I know if there was not a big flood that had submerged all the lands on earth? I did not want to believe it. But what evidence did I have to convince myself of the contrary? How long did Noah stay at sea without seeing land? Wasn't it forty-four days? How long had we been at sea? Forty-five days?

<u>July 22, 1955</u>
Ship's Position 44°47'N 156°57'W, Wind nil, Temp 15°C

We were becalmed. There was not even a breeze. The sky was clear. The sun was warm. We took our beddings out on deck and spread them on the furled sails, anchor hawser, cabin top, bamboo battens, wherever we could find a space to air them.

At noon we sighted a ship over the horizon. Our spirits were elevated like Noah seeing one of his doves returning to the ark with a piece of straw in its beak. That was the only man-made object we had seen for the past 46 days. At first she did not notice us. She kept her course. Then we remembered the flag. As soon as we hoisted it up, she changed course. When she got close enough to see what was on our flag, all her crew showed up on her deck. From the last word in her name, California Maru, we could tell that she was Japanese. We were surprised to hear Chinese spoken to us through a loud speaker:

"Need any help?"

We could not believe that the Jolly Roger really worked as Cal's friend, Ann Rohrer, had told us.

"No," Marco yelled back. Shouldn't ships talk to one another when passing on high sea? "Where are you bound for?"

"San Francisco."

Hearing these words brought me back to believe that there was land beyond that horizon. Were we in the shipping lane? We had better pay more attention to watch out that no one ran into us.

July 23, 1955

Ship's Position 44°30'N 156°15'W, Wind S 1 B.S., Distance sailed: 45 miles during the last 24 hours. Two miles an hour!

We have been at sea for 36 days. Provisions were only 1/3 consumed. With captain's strict rationing, our fresh water supply should hold up for another month. Patience was running thin and abrasive. Every little subject would bring up an argument. When Benny started the auxiliary engine to charge the battery, Reno said the smell of the exhaust reminded him of the diesel bus in the French Concession in Shanghai.

"That bus was run on gasoline, not diesel," Huloo correction him.

"Definitely diesel! I could tell from its smell."

Pretty soon everyone joined in. I could bet that even if we could go to Shanghai now and found out what it was, diesel or gasoline, the losers would argue that six years ago it was not that way.

At least the argument broke the monotony.

July 24, 1955

Ship's Position 44°10'N 154°20'W, Wind WSW 3 B.S., Distance sailed noon to noon 85 miles

It was my day for cooking. The rice came out half cooked and half raw. Everyone complained about not being able to swallow.

"You don't have to swallow," I said. "Just drink some water and let gravity bring it down."

"Swallow is not a result of gravitation," Huloo said. "It is a contraction of muscles."

"Why do you think the mouth is on top of the stomach?"

"It does not have to be that way. One can still swallow if the mouth is below the stomach."

"What are you talking about?"

"I don't just talk. I can prove it."

"Prove it."

Huloo filled his mug and went to his bunk. Then in front of all of us, he emptied the entire mug of water into his stomach while standing on his head. Not a single drop had spilled out.

July 25, 1955

Ship's Position 43°23'N 150°21'W, Wind SSW 3 B.S., Temp 16°C

The reason to have two transmitters on board was that the chance of both of them break down at the same time was almost nil. But it happened. I could not make contact with KFS for two days already.

"Pound on it," Reno suggested.

"How can pounding help?" I asked. "It will make it worse."

"If they do not work, what do you care if they get worse? The worst is they still do not work."

As I was hesitating, Reno hit both of them with his palm. As I had expected, it did not work. Then he climbed onto the rice sack and kicked them. Amazingly one of them worked!

As soon as I established contact with KFS, these letters rapped out of my receiver in codes:

WHAT HAPPENED PAUL

I tapped:

TRANSMITTER OUT

The reply came back:

GIVE IT A KICK

I went:

HOW YOU THINK I GOT ON

He went:

WHATS UP

Here went my message:

NR.69 CK31 JUNK FREE CHINA 261155GMT 6056 TAIPEI

4323N 15021W 1031MB 16C WIND WSW3 BEEN
MAKING LITTLE PROGRESS FOR WHOLE WEEK
WITH INSUFFICIENT WIND COULD NOT CONTACT
KFS FOR TWO DAYS DUE TO LOOSE WIRING INSIDE
RADIO ALL WELL

While we were taking turns to stand watch, our chickens were
also taking turns to lay eggs. They had been faithfully giving us
one egg every day. But Huloo suspected that only one of them was
laying the eggs.

"Which one?" Marco asked.

"The one being pecked on by the other one. See, she has
hardly any feather left of her head."

"How do you know?"

"I gave them the finger test every morning."

"Then let's eat the guilty one," Reno suggested.

"The other one is bound to lay eggs sooner or later," was
Huloo's response.

We took turn in eating the eggs. Where could one find eggs so
fresh? They were still warm. So we poked two holes, one at each
end, and sucked the content out. But Cal refused to do so. He
always made a big production in frying it when it was his turn.

"I think we should give our chicken names," Cal suggested
after he finished eating his fried egg in front of five pairs of
envying eyes. We all looked at him as if he was crazy.

"Names for chicken?" Benny asked.

"Yes, don't you name your pets?"

"Pets?"

"Americans think pets are members of their families."

"Since when did they become our pets?" Marco raised the
question.

"When we get to San Francisco, the first thing people would
ask when they see the chicken is their names."

"They can ask all what they want. We don't have to answer
them," I said.

"How about Mildred?"

"For both of them?"

"Then how about Mildred I and Mildred II?"

"That's like taking off your pants to fart."

"What do you mean, Huloo?"

"Much ado about nothing," explained Reno.

July 26, 1955

Ship's Position 43°36'N 147°35'W, Wind NNW 3 B.S., Temp 14°C, Overcast

Our uninvited passengers were getting bolder. They came out at night to chase after each other. Last night some even ran over my blanket. Tonight I waited with a fist under the blanket. Sure enough, one of them landed on my blanket. I hit the blanket as hard as I could. It felt as if I had hit a home run. Everyone heard the squealing, followed by a thump as it hit the deck. Applause broke out in the dark. That ought to teach them a lesson.

Huloo's cage did not catch any rat. Why would they go for the canned meat in his cage when they had all the rice and flour and beans they could eat to their hearts' content?

"Now wash your face before you go to bed," the captain told his crew. "I don't want to see anyone losing his nose in the morning."

Well, the junk was only so big. We'll just have to co-exist with them. Should we consider them our shipmates as we did to our two chickens? Should we put them on our crew's list to show the customs when we made port?

"Hey, Cal, you want to give them names?"

"How many of them are there?"

July 27, 1955

Ship's position 43°25'N 146°30'W

We received a surprise telegram from the Chinese consulate in San Francisco asking for our ETA. The best I could give them was EARLY AUGUST.

It was Huloo's day to cook. He surprised us by serving fresh bean sprouts.

"Is that from your vegetable garden?" Cal asked.

"You city people! Bean sprouts don't grow. They sprout."

"What do they sprout from?"

"Beans."

"Where did you get the fertilizer?"

"No fertilizer. Just water."

"I'll be damned!"

"That's right. All the early Western seafarers were damned by scurvy caused by the deficiency of vitamin C."

"Western seafarers only?"

"Yes, the Chinese sailors were never short of vitamin C. They drank green tea and ate fresh bean sprouts at sea."

"I'll be... ta-ma-de!"

July 28, 1955

Ship's Position 43°19'N 145°34'W, Wind NW 3 B.S., Distance sailed 45 miles

The Chinese consulate's request for an ETA reminded us that we were going to make port pretty soon. Huloo gave haircuts to everybody and I gave one to Huloo that caused him to curse me for the rest of the day. Cal refused to take one.

"At least shave off that bushy beard," Marco said to him.

"I really don't understand you guys," he shook his head and said. "After a long rough trip like this, you are supposed to look rugged and worn out, not neat and trimmed."

July 29, 1955

We received another telegram from the Consulate. They were not satisfied with our answer. They wanted a definite time and date of arrival so that they could organize a welcoming party. What could we tell them when we had no idea what the wind was going to be like? Were they Chinese? Did they know that traveling depended on wind? The Chinese say "Fair wind" instead of "Goodbye" when they saw someone off on a trip.

July 30, 1955

Ship's Position 43°05'N 141°40'W, Wind WNW 4 B.S., Temp

13°C

Shortened sail, on starboard tack most of the time. We were finally leaving the "Prevailing Wind" and, hopefully, to catch the coastal wind on the American continent. We changed course and headed for Farallon, the landfall I had planned on making.

I came on deck and climbed to the highest thwart on the fantail to try to get a shot of the sun with my sextant as the junk was riding up and down on the high waves.

"Our Father who art in the Heaven..." Reno was singing on the tiller while Cal was standing next to him on the lookout.

"Are you a Christian, Reno?" Cal asked.

"No."

"Where did you learn that song? It's the Lord's Prayer."

"I learned it from the movie *Student Prince.* It was sung by Mario Lanza."

"By the way it's *In Heaven,* not *In the Heaven,*" Cal corrected him.

"You understand what I said?"

"Yes."

"Then what is all that fuss about THE or no THE?"

Cal shut up and walked to the starboard side. He unbuttoned his pants. He paused and noticed the wind. Then he walked across the boat to the port side.

"Way to go!" Reno said.

"*The way to go,* not *way to go,*" Cal corrected him again.

"You understand what I said?"

"Yes, but that's not how we say it in English. In Chinese you don't have to worry about articles, genders and tenses."

"Says who? We used to have all those junks you now have in English. But we are smarter. When we found them meaningless and cumbersome, we got rid of them. That is why the Chinese today is so concise. If I have already told you that something took place yesterday, why do I have to constantly use a past tense in redundancy? Do you know how many different YOU, the second person pronoun, the Chinese used to have? Ni, ru, er, jun and I don't know how many more. Each one is used in a specific situation. Now we have gotten rid of all of them except one, the one you know NI. How could you English speaking people stand to carry this baggage for such a long time? You watch, sooner or later you will wise up and get rid of them."

"Go away, Reno!"

July 31, 1955

Ship's Position 43°16'N 138°48'W, Wind W 4 B.S., Temp 14°C, Sea rough

I turned on the radio to get in touch with KFS. Somehow the codes coming out of it sounded strange. I could not pinpoint what was wrong. So I tapped in

WHERE IS GEORGE

The answer was

GEORGE CALLED IN SICK TODAY I AM JOHN

Suddenly I realized that Morse Code had a voice. John's voice was distinctively different from that of George. I sure missed George.

August 1, 1955

730 miles to San Francisco, Ship's Position 42°51'N 136°28'W, Temp 13°C, Becalmed,

It's my birthday. I received a message from my uncle:

PAUL CHOW JUNK FREE CHINA KSF

APPRECIATE YOUR THOUGHTFUL RADIOGRAM ALSO INFORMATIONS THROUGH MACKAY'S KINDNESS IF SHIRLEY FAILS TO WELCOME YOU BEFORE LEAVING FRISCO AROUND AUGUST SIXTH MY LETTER WILL AWAIT YOU CARE MACKAY LOVE PAO

I woke up this morning and realized it was my day to have the egg. That got me out of bed immediately and rushed to the poop deck. I was shocked to see Huloo killing a chicken.

"What are you doing, Huloo?"

"Can't you see?"

"Didn't you say sooner or later she will give us eggs?"

"But this is your birthday."

"Which one did you kill, Mildred I or Mildred II?"

"Who cares?"

"You could have killed the one that is laying the golden eggs."

"I'm not stupid. I gave them finger tests beforehand."

"Then where is my egg?"

"I confiscated it."

"You what?"

"I need it for making the egg-flower soup."

It was the best dinner we had ever had on the entire voyage. It tasted even better than the banquet the overseas Chinese in Japan gave us on our arrival. The captain suspended the prohibition rule at sea. We drank the beer Lao Tu, Marco's drinking friend in Yokosuka, gave us. Even Benny and Huloo drank.

August 2, 1955

Ship's Position 42°50'N 136°19'W, Temp 14°C, Becalmed for 21 hours. In the afternoon we finally got some wind from the NE direction at 2 Beauford scale (roughly 15 miles an hour).

I did not have my egg yesterday. So it was still my turn. But no egg today.

August 3, 1955

Ship's Position 42°17'N 135°21'W, Temp 15°C, 1035MB, Wind N/E 3 B.S.

We got another message from the Consulate. They wanted a story of our voyage for publicity. We asked Cal to write one. He had been very imaginary in suggesting American falling overboard and sea serpent coming out of the fog. But what he gave us was nothing like that. They were the mundane daily life on board such as standing watch and cooking, the chicken and the navigator's birthday party, the boredom in the calm and the American studying Chinese, reading from William Faulkner to Mickey Spillane, except that he did have a lengthy description of the captain falling overboard, which I had refused to send to the newspapers.

I was still waiting for my egg. But there was still no egg.

August 4, 1955

350 miles to Farallon, 375 miles to go to reach San Francisco, Ship's Position 40°54'N 131°35'W, Wind N 5 B.S., Temp 15°C, rough sea, the main sheets broke twice, sailing at half sail, making a speed of 5 knots, distance covered from noon to noon 147 nautical miles, the second best after 178 miles made on July 8.

Still no egg this morning.

"Did you kill the wrong chicken, Huloo?" I asked.

"Absolutely not," Huloo answered with absolute certainty. "I told you I gave the finger tests beforehand."

"Then why no eggs?"

"I guess chickens are human too. I should not have killed it in front of the other one. Or it could be caused by loneliness."

"You mean it misses being pecked on by the other one?"

"I don't know."

"You still think you can sail across the Pacific all by yourself?"

"I am not a chicken," Huloo said.

Cal asked me to send a message to his boss Dr. Bodman in Taiwan:

NR76 CK34 JUNK FREE CHINA BEDM 040600GMT
6056 TAIPEI
PAA TO AMERICAN EMBASSY DOCTOR BODMAN
BODMAN FLOATING LANGUAGE INSTITUTE 500
MILES FROM GOLDEN GATE TOTAL 6000 MILES 1200
FLASH CARDS INSTITUTE FACULTY AND STUDENT
RETURN TAIWAN ABOUT ONE SEPTEMBER MEHLERT

August 5, 1955

330 miles to Farallon, Ship's Position 40°14'N 129°13'W, Wind N 5 B.S., Speed 5 knots under half sail, Temp 17°C

"What is that?" someone pointed to the water and asked. That brought everybody on deck. It was some brownish yellowish stalk with large leaves. There was not just one. As we sailed along they kept appearing in the water. Then we passed one right next to our side. We picked it up and pulled it on board. But we could never get to its end. It finally broke off. It filled our entire foredeck, all thirty feet of it.

"That's kelp," Cal said.

"What's kelp?"

"See weeds."

"Seaweeds could never to seen so far away from shore."

"Don't you eat seaweeds in China?"

"They don't come so big. I wonder if fish in America are also bigger than those on the China coast."

August 6, 1955

209 miles to Farallon, 234 miles to SF, Ship's Position 39°21'N 126°34'W, Wind N 5 B.S., Temp 15°C, Sea rough, Speed 5 knots under half sail,

After spending 68 days at sea in gale weather and calms and sailing in a zigzag course that covered 5868 nautical miles, I had some confidence to make an estimate on sailing time for the rest of 234 miles. I informed the Harbor Master of San Francisco with the following message:

NR81 CK21 JUNK FREE CHINA BEDM 062000GMT
HARBOR MASTER SAN FRANCISCO HARBOR
209 MILES TO FARALLON ETA SAN FRANCISCO
AUGUST8 1300 PROVIDED WIND PREVAILS MASTER
JUNK FREE CHINA

The message somehow got into the hands of the Chinese Consulate people in San Francisco. They did not like the condition of wind we had stated in the message. They insisted to have a firm time so that they could organize a welcoming party at the dockside. They finally agree to accept a "more reliable ETA" 24 hours in advance of our arrival. If we could not arrive on time, would I be flogged, fined or put in jail?

August 7, 1955

Ship's Position 38°48'N 124°06'W, 20 miles SW/W of Pt.

Arena, wind nil

"Ta-ma-de where is the wind?" I swore after the wind died completely.

"Where are we?" Cal asked.

"We should have been 5 miles off Pt. Reyes by now if that damn wind did not die on us this morning."

"That's where my brother Charles is."

"What do you mean?"

"My brother is a park ranger at Tamales Bay State Park right next to Pt. Reyes."

"You mean a park?"

"Yes, a park."

"In what city?"

"It's far away from any city."

"Then why the fish ponds and flowers? Who's going to see them?"

"There are no fish ponds or flowers in American state or national parks."

"What do they have?"

"Nothing. They were kept just as they were found, wilderness."

"You call that a park?"

"Yes, can you send a telegram to Charlie for me?"

Here was the telegram we sent to Cal's brother:

NR85 CK21 JUNK FREE CHINA COLLECT 071200GMT
CHARLES MEHLERT INVERNESS CALIFORNIA
PASS POINT REYES EARLY MORNING MONDAY
SANFRANCISOCO AFTERNOON WIND PREVAILING
CREW JUNK FREE CHINA SENDS GREETING CALVIN

San Francisco tomorrow? But there was no wind in sight. In the meantime, we received another telegram from the Chinese Consulate in San Francisco asking us for a last firm ETA with no more "wishy-washy" changes. I thought I should play it safe to give them two ETAs.

ETA LIGHTSHIP AT NOON
ETA GOLDEN GATE 3PM

Paul Chow

While waiting for the wind, the captain ordered a boat cleaning. We cleaned the entire inside of the cabin and our bunks. While we were cleaning the outside of the cabin, Marco went into the storage hold and took out all the old ropes that we had replaced from our rigging. Before we could figure out what he was going to do with them, he started to throw them overboard.

"Are you going out of your mind?" Huloo, the sail master who was supposed to be in charge of ropes and sails, jumped up and cried in fury. "Stop that!"

It was too late. Most of them were already gone.

"If you throw away even another little piece of string, I'll throw you overboard!" Huloo threatened in anger. I had never seen Huloo so mad. He might just do what he had said.

Marco acted as if he had not heard Huloo. He went back into the hold and brought on deck all the paints we had left from the restoration of the junk back in Keelung. I held my breath and waited to see a storm to explode.

"Let's paint the cabin," Marco said. That made all the heads turn to him with mysterious looks. None of us had ever heard of painting at sea. Perhaps they did it on the big merchant ships to occupy their deckhands, but never on fishing boats. No one paid any attention to Marco except Cal. For a great part of the calm, we watched the two of them paint the entire outside of the cabin.

The wind whipped up after dark. By eight o'clock it had grown to a gale force. The junk was flying at 9 knots at the least. Huloo, Benny and I wanted to shorten the sails. Marco, Reno and Cal wanted to keep them up in full. As usual, we put up a heated argument. Marco finally withdrew his support for a full sail. We reefed. We were still making good speed under half sail. In just a few short hours we recovered all the miles we had lost in the calm during the day. We all retired to our bunks leaving only those on watch on deck. Then that deadly voice pierced into the cabin,

"Top main sheets broke off!"

We heaved to. Huloo walked up the battens to tie up the sheets. When he came down on the top of the cabin, he slipped and fell. The junk had already got on a tack. The sheets were tight and off to the side. He had nothing to hold on. He got up and fell again. Huloo was a taichi master. Instead of getting up again on a rolling deck, he rolled himself skillfully off the cabin top. He was all white from the wet paint that Marco and Cal had painted on the cabin. He walked over to Marco and punched his chest.

"Bi-yang-de! You landlubber! Painting at sea."

Marco was big. He was not moved by Huloo's punch. He did not move in his emotion either. He just put up his usual laugh and said, "Ha, ha, ha, ha, don't get so excited, Huloo. I'll clean that paint off your clothes for you."

Huloo shook off Marco's hand from his shoulder and said,

"From now on you are no more the captain of this boat! At least not for me. You don't behave like one."

August 8, 1955

15 nautical mile to San Francisco, Ship's Position 37°47'N 122°50'W,

I stayed up all night, going between the poop deck and the chart table. While I was trying to push for the last mile to the landfall I expected to make, the reefs of Dongsha kept creeping up in my mind. There supposed to be a lighthouse on it. But I couldn't see anything in this foggy night. I had already put one boat on Donsha back then, I said to myself, I couldn't afford to lose this one now.

That's it.

"All hands on deck!" I woke everybody up.

"What happened?" asked the sleepy voices.

"Let's douse the sails."

"What do you mean?" Reno questioned. "We are making good speed."

"Douse right now!"

As usual, the crew got into an argument. I had no time to lose. Seamanlike or not seamanlike, I grabbed the tiller from the helmsman and pushed it all the way alee. I secured it to the bulwark. The junk swung nicely around and came to a dead stop.

"Why did you do that for?" the helmsman was angered by my

rude interference.

"I don't want to put her on the rock."

"What rock?"

"SE Farallon."

"Are you sure we are there?" Marco asked.

"Not sure."

"Then why stop?"

"Because I'm not sure."

"What shall we do now?"

"Wait for daylight."

"There are two more hours to daylight."

"As long as it takes, we'll wait."

Being heaved to in a strong wind reminded me of being disabled in Typhoon Annie. The difference was we could not afford to drop a sea anchor this time. We would have no time to hoist it up in case Farallon showed up right in front of us. We would just have to ride it out. The uncontrolled rolling made me seasick.

Daylight finally arrived with a heavy fog. We have everyone on the lookout through the fog. Suddenly out of the fog a boat appeared on our starboard bow. It was a fishing boat about two third our size. It was so close that we could see the man on the wheel on the topside. We waved and hailed like a bunch of bushmen coming out of the wilderness. The man did not pay any attention to us. He stopped the engine and dashed down below. I immediately knew what he was going to do. I ran into the cabin and turned my receiver to the fishermen's band. I heard a frantic voice,

"I have been out only two days. Just a minute ago I almost collide into a Chinese junk with two large gawking eyeballs looking at me. Where am I?"

Too bad I couldn't talk on my Collins TCS-13 transmitter. I went back on the poop deck. The fisherman was already on the topside. I hollered,

"Where is SE Farallon?"

"You are right next to it," the man warned. "Don't move!"

"Can't see it."

"You'll see it when the fog lifts in about an hour or so."

Then he went down to the deck and climbed into his hold. A few seconds later, he came back up with a big fish. With both hands holding it, he swung his body. A shiny silvery fish landed on our deck.

"Welcome to San Francisco!" he yelled before returning to the topside. Then as suddenly as she had appeared, the fishing boat disappeared into the fog.

8:15am The fog lifted to reveal a towering black rock above our masts. Angry waves were trying to climb onto it. White foams were running off its face. Some brownish animals were clinging to the small rocks at the foot of the cliff.

"Look, what are those?" Benny asked.

"Sea lions," said Cal.

"How do you know?"

"They are natives of San Francisco just like me."

We raised our sail and steered NE/E for San Francisco Bay, making 4 knots under a good breeze.

12:00pm We came within half a mile to the Lightship outside of San Francisco. A little while later the wind weakened. The sky cleared up except a low-lying layer of cloud over the shore in the distance. Under the white blanket there was a long bright red structure connecting the two ends of the distant shore. Its tops were hidden in the cloud. Is that the Golden Gate Bridge?

All of a sudden, my anxiety was deflated. All those worries about the wind being too strong for the mast and the battens or being too weak for us to make any headway, the sea being too rough on the tiller and the poor visibility that blocked the horizon, the sun, the stars, Iro Saki, Kimomoto Shima, Farallon, ... etc. seemed so trivial. If six inexperienced coastal fishermen could make it on a 50-year junk with no modern equipments but a compass and a sexton, there left absolutely no doubt in our minds that many of our more experienced seafaring ancestors must have made across this ocean at their doorstep on larger boats before us.

Now my only worry was:

"Is that bridge tall enough to clear our masts?"

That was not the navigator's job. Leaving it for the captain to worry about, I went into the cabin and sent out my last radio message:

NR91 CK27 KFS DE BEDM 081900GMT
LAST MESSAGE FROM JUNK FREE CHINA
HALF MILE FROM LIGHTSHIP BREEZE DIMINISH
MAKING ONLY 2KNTS TOWARD GOLDEN GATE
ETA SF 2PM ALL WELL ITS BEEN GREAT
PLEASURE TALKING WITH YOU GEORGE
JUNK FREE CHINA SIGNS OFF

Oakland Tribune

ASSOCIATED PRESS...WIREPHOTO...WIDE WORLD...UNITED PRESS...CHICAGO DAILY NEWS FOREIGN SERVICE

OAKLAND'S
LOCALLY OWNED AND
LOCALLY CONTROLLED
DAILY NEWSPAPER

VOL. CLXIII   OAKLAND, CALIFORNIA, TUESDAY, AUGUST 9, 1955   17 ₱ ★   NO. 40

Junk Reaches S.F. After Epic Voyage

'Free China' With Six Aboard Completes Trip From Formosa

By HARRY OFLAHERTY

A sail had looked like a buddy heading westward, heading through the fog off the Golden Gate.

Moments later a floating complex of lumber adorned with two ungainly dragon's eyes as visible beneath the sail.

Then — early — before 4 p.m., yesterday the junk "Free China," with six aboard ended an epic 6,000-mile voyage from Formosa to California and another wonderful chapter in the story of navigation had been written.

Three manned were Marco V. Lee, Captain, skipper of the junk; Reno, yellow-painted junk; Paul C. L. Crow, Los Cel He, Reno Chu-Lang Chen, Chia-Chen Hu, and Calvin E. Mehlert, 22, of Fresno, U.S. Vice Consul in the Foreign Service.

And a chicken named "Nhuong."

About the Author

Paul Chow grew up in the family of a government railroad manager. Throughout his childhood, his family moved with his father's career, from one railroad line to another. In 1937, Japan invaded China, shattering the life of this family. His mother, with four children in tow, ran for their lives, keeping barely one step ahead of the advancing enemy forces. With WWII on the doorsteps, Chow quit high school to join the Allied Forces in Burma to fight the Japanese, which by that time had occupied most of Southeast Asia. After the war, he took up fishing. But after spending nine years at sea, fisherman's life offered little challenge to him. In 1955, he bought a junk and sailed across the Pacific Ocean with five of his friends. At the age of 29, having been through fourteen different schools and no high school diploma to speak of, he enrolled in a junior college in San Francisco. After a bachelor's degree from the University of California at Berkeley he went on to obtain a PhD from Northwestern University. For the next 29 years he taught physics and astronomy in universities and did consulting in computer industry. Since retirement from California State University at Northridge in 1994, Chow has devoted full time to writing.

8314714R0

Made in the USA
Charleston, SC
27 May 2011